Key Geography Interactions

David Waugh
Former Head of Geography
Trinity School
Carlisle

Tony Bushell
Head of Geography
West Gate Community College
Newcastle upon Tyne

Stanley Thornes (Publishers) Ltd

Second edition designed and reset by Hilary Norman
Illustrations by Kathy Baxendale, Mike Gordon, Hardlines and Tim Smith
Edited by Katherine James
Photo research by Elisabeth Savery

First edition published in 1993 and reprinted 7 times by:
Stanley Thornes (Publishers) Ltd
Ellenborough House
Wellington Street
CHELTENHAM GL50 1YW
England

97 98 99 00 01 / 10 9 8 7 6 5 4 3 2 1

A catalogue record of this book is available from the British Library.

ISBN 0-7487-3030-3

Printed and bound in Hong Kong

The previous page shows the Japanese bullet train with Mt Fuji in the background

Acknowledgements

The authors and publishers are grateful to the following for permission to reproduce photographs and other material in this book:

Art Directors (p. 57 top right); Bruce Coleman Ltd (pp. 58, 60 bottom left); Countryside Commission (pp. 42, 43); Eye Ubiquitous (pp. 62 bottom, 66, 67, 73 top left); Fiat UK Ltd (p. 65); J & E Forder (p. 101 bottom); Geoscience Features Picture Library (pp. 22, 30); Robert Harding Picture Library (pp. 9, 15 top right, 19 right, 57 left, 61 top, 79, 80 top); Hulton Getty (p. 94 top); Hutchison Library (pp. 32 top, 40 top, 57 bottom right, 73 top right, 88 left); ICCE Photo Library (pp. 11); Image Bank (p. 64); Impact (p. 63 right); Japan Information Centre (p. 72); Japan Ship Centre (p. 75); Mazda Motor Corporation (pp. 76, 77); National Trust Photolibrary (p. 101 top); Network (p. 63 left); Olivier Negrie (p. 52 bottom left); Panos Pictures (pp. 78 bottom left, 91); Rex Features/Sipa Press (p. 53); Science Photo Library (pp. 24, 80 bottom right, 94 bottom, 95 top); Spectrum Colour Library (p. 49 right); Still Pictures (pp. 8, 32 bottom, 34); Sygma (p. 23); Peter Thornton (p. 99); Tony Stone

Images (pp. 1, 15 top left, bottom right, 60 top left, 61 bottom right, 73 centre, 88 bottom right); Topham Picture Source (p. 25); The Walt Disney Company (pp. 50, 51 all); World Pictures (pp. 16, 40 bottom, 49 left, 60 centre).

All other photographs were supplied by the authors.

Every effort has been made to contact copyright holders and we apologise if any have been overlooked.

Contents

What factors affect climate?

Can you remember the difference between weather and climate shown on diagram **A**? There are several types of climate found across the world. Each type has its own distinctive pattern of temperature and rainfall.

Several factors affect climate. Four of these factors are **latitude**, the **distance from the sea**, **prevailing winds** and major **relief** features. It is important to understand these factors before looking at Britain's climate and comparing it with other places in the world.

Weather is the day to day condition of the atmosphere. It includes temperature, precipitation and wind.

The **climate** of a place is its average weather taken over many years.

A

B

Latitude

Places near the Equator are hotter than places near the poles. This is due mainly to the curvature of the earth and the angle of the sun.

At the Equator the sun is often overhead. It shines straight down and its heat is concentrated on a small area which gets very hot.

Towards the poles the sun shines more at an angle. Its heat is spread over a larger area and temperatures are lower.

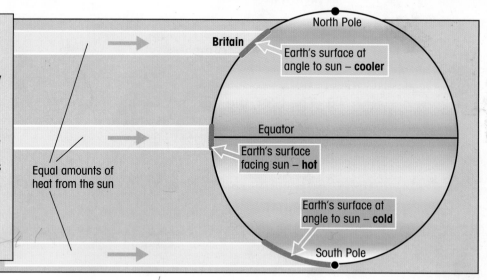

North Pole

Britain

Earth's surface at angle to sun – **cooler**

Equal amounts of heat from the sun

Equator

Earth's surface facing sun – **hot**

Earth's surface at angle to sun – **cold**

South Pole

C

Distance from the sea

The distance a place is from the sea affects its temperature (diagram **C**). In summer places which are inland and away from the sea are usually warmer than places near to the coast. In winter it is usually the opposite with inland places being cooler than places near to the coast.

Imagine you have to do the washing up at home and there is no hot water. You fill a kettle with cold water and have to wait for a few **minutes** for it to heat up. You put the hot water and some cutlery in a bowl. Within **seconds** the cutlery becomes hot. After washing, the cutlery cools down in a few seconds but the water in the bowl stays warm for much longer. This is because liquids, like the sea, take longer to heat up than solids like the land. Once warm, liquids keep their heat for much longer than solids.

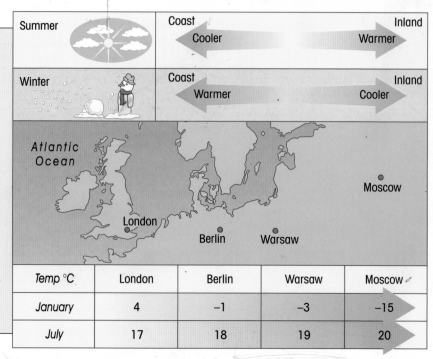

Summer

Coast — Inland

Cooler ← → Warmer

Winter

Coast — Inland

Warmer ← → Cooler

Atlantic Ocean

Moscow

London

Berlin   Warsaw

Temp °C	London	Berlin	Warsaw	Moscow
January	4	−1	−3	−15
July	17	18	19	20

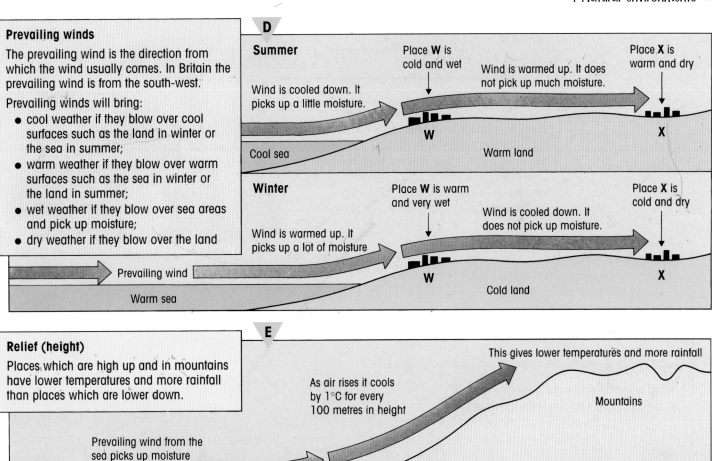

Prevailing winds

The prevailing wind is the direction from which the wind usually comes. In Britain the prevailing wind is from the south-west.

Prevailing winds will bring:
- cool weather if they blow over cool surfaces such as the land in winter or the sea in summer;
- warm weather if they blow over warm surfaces such as the sea in winter or the land in summer;
- wet weather if they blow over sea areas and pick up moisture;
- dry weather if they blow over the land

Relief (height)

Places which are high up and in mountains have lower temperatures and more rainfall than places which are lower down.

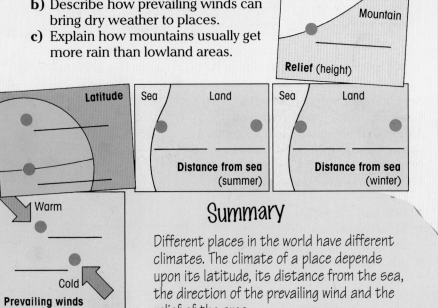

Activities

1 What is the difference between weather and climate?

2 a) Make a copy of the five diagrams in **F**.
b) Each diagram shows two places. Write **warmer** or **cooler** at each place.
c) Write the correct sentence from the following list under each diagram.
- The sea keeps coastal places cool.
- Temperature is affected by the direction from which the wind comes.
- Temperature decreases with height.
- Places near the Equator are warmer because of the overhead sun.
- The sea keeps coastal places warm.

3 With the help of labelled diagrams:
a) Describe how prevailing winds can bring wet weather to places.
b) Describe how prevailing winds can bring dry weather to places.
c) Explain how mountains usually get more rain than lowland areas.

Summary

Different places in the world have different climates. The climate of a place depends upon its latitude, its distance from the sea, the direction of the prevailing wind and the relief of the area.

5

What is Britain's climate?

The graph in diagram **B** shows the average monthly temperatures and rainfall for a place in Britain. The reasons why Britain has this type of climate are given beside the graph. You may have to turn back to pages 4 and 5 for their explanation.

Britain usually has cool summers and mild winters

Although rain can fall at any time of the year, winters are usually wetter than summers

A

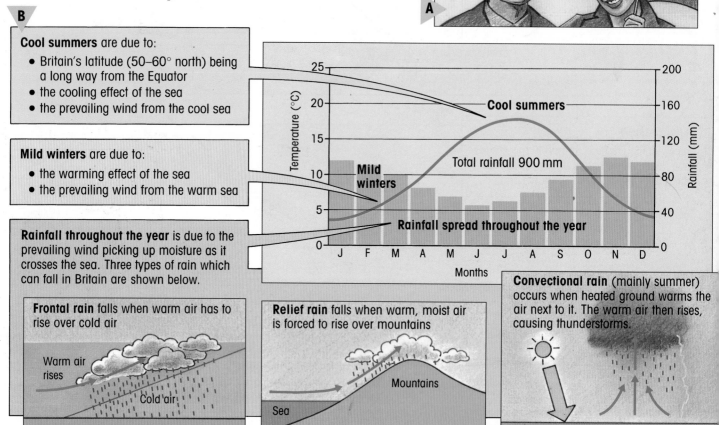

B

Cool summers are due to:
- Britain's latitude (50–60° north) being a long way from the Equator
- the cooling effect of the sea
- the prevailing wind from the cool sea

Mild winters are due to:
- the warming effect of the sea
- the prevailing wind from the warm sea

Rainfall throughout the year is due to the prevailing wind picking up moisture as it crosses the sea. Three types of rain which can fall in Britain are shown below.

Cool summers

Total rainfall 900 mm

Mild winters

Rainfall spread throughout the year

Months

Frontal rain falls when warm air has to rise over cold air

Warm air rises

Cold air

Relief rain falls when warm, moist air is forced to rise over mountains

Mountains

Sea

Convectional rain (mainly summer) occurs when heated ground warms the air next to it. The warm air then rises, causing thunderstorms.

What other parts of the world have a 'British' climate?

Several other parts of the world have a similar type of climate to Britain. Although their climate is not exactly the same, they do have cool summers, mild winters and rain throughout the year. These places are shown on map **C**.

Notice that these places:
- lie between latitudes 40° and 60° north or south of the Equator
- are mostly on the west coast of continents
- have prevailing winds coming from the west, i.e. from the sea
- have mountains inland from the coast.

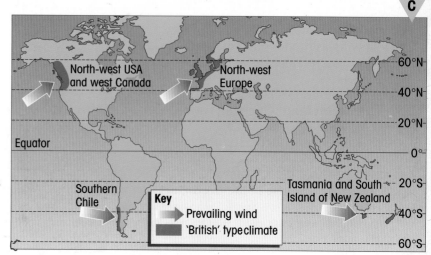

C

North-west USA and west Canada

North-west Europe

Equator

Southern Chile

Tasmania and South Island of New Zealand

Key
→ Prevailing wind
■ 'British' type climate

How does the climate differ in other parts of the world?

D

Canadian Arctic
In this part of the world it is always very cold, with a lot of snow in winter

British Isles
I can never be sure what our weather will be like. It is usually cool in summer, mild in winter and it often rains.

The Mediterranean
Where I live we get hot, dry summers and mild, wet winters

Amazon Basin, Brazil
Where I live it is very hot and very wet all year

Kenya
Our weather is warm all year. We get rain in summer but it is dry in winter.

Sahara Desert
I am used to every day being very hot and dry

In the remainder of this unit we will look at the weather conditions for three of these different types of climate. We will also see how the climate affects the vegetation of each area.

Activities

1 Copy out and complete the sentence below:

The British Isles have _____ summers, _____ winters and _____ throughout the year.

2 Name four places in the world which have the same type of climate as Britain.

3 Which **four** of the following statements are correct about the British climate?
- Summers are cool because Britain is a long way from the Equator.
- Summers are hot because the sun is overhead.
- Winters are mild due to warm winds blowing from the sea.
- Winters are mild because Britain is near to the Equator.
- Rain falls all year because winds blow from the sea.
- Britain gets frontal and relief rainfall all year, and convectional rainfall in summer.

Summary

The British climate has mild winters and cool summers, and rain falls throughout the year.

What is the equatorial climate?

Graph **A** shows the **equatorial** type of climate. It is hot and wet throughout the year. Rainfall is heavy and falls during most afternoons. There are no winters or summers (seasons) like there are in Britain. One day is very similar to the next.

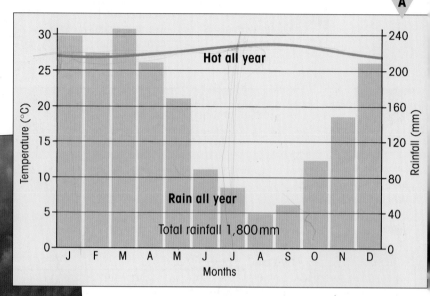

A

Hot all year

Rain all year

Total rainfall 1,800 mm

B

Thunderstorm above the rainforest

The daily pattern

The weather in Britain changes from day to day. In equatorial areas the weather is far more predictable. The weather pattern described below is likely to be repeated day after day for most of the year.

C

Time	Weather conditions
6.00 a.m. (0600)	Sun rises as always at this time. No clouds in sky.
7.00 a.m. (0700)	Gets warmer. Very little wind.
8.00 a.m. (0800)	Temperature 25°C (same as a warm summer afternoon in England)
9.00 a.m. (0900)	Temperature continues to rise. Becomes very hot as the
10.00 a.m. (1000)	sun gets higher in the sky. Hot air rises. Water
11.00 a.m. (1100)	from rivers, swamps and vegetation evaporates.
Midday	Temperature reaches 33°C. Sun overhead. Hot air continues to rise.
1.00 p.m. (1300)	Water vapour carried high into sky. Cools and condenses to form white cumulus clouds.
2.00 p.m. (1400)	Clouds increase in size and height. Turn into towering dark grey cumulo-nimbus rainclouds.
3.00 p.m. (1500)	Torrential rainstorm with thunder and lightning.
4.00 p.m. (1600)	Storm continues.
5.00 p.m. (1700)	Storm ends. Clouds begin to break up.
6.00 p.m. (1800)	Sun sets. The night is clear and calm.

Which places have an equatorial climate?

Map **D** shows this type of climate to be mainly limited to places within 5° north or south of the Equator. The two main areas where it is found are the huge river basins of the Amazon in South America and the Zaire in Africa. The major factor which affects this climate is its latitude. The sun is overhead throughout the year. This gives high temperatures and is responsible for the convectional rainfall. There is no prevailing wind and the air is calm apart from during thunderstorms.

How can height affect different places with the same latitude?

However, not all places near to the Equator have this type of climate. This is because of **altitude**. In East Africa two mountains, Kilimanjaro and Kenya, rise to nearly 6,000 metres (19,000 feet). Two South American volcanoes, Cotopaxi and Chimborazo, rise to similar heights in the Andes. As photo **E** of Mount Kenya shows, this makes it cold enough for snow to lie all year on the mountain summits.

D

Amazon Basin · Zaire Basin · Mt Kenya · Indonesia
Equator · Mt Cotopaxi · Mt Chimborazo · Mt Kilimanjaro
5°N · 0° · 5°S

◼ Equatorial climate ▲ Volcano

E Mount Kenya

Activities

1 Write out the paragraph below choosing the correct word from the pair in brackets.

> The equatorial climate is (hot/warm) and (dry/wet) all year. Rainfall is (heavy/light) and falls during most (mornings/afternoons). The weather for each day of the year is very (different/similar).

2 Look at map **D**. Which **two** of the statements below correctly describe the location of the equatorial climate?
- It is mainly found between latitudes 5°N and 5°S of the Equator.
- All places on the Equator have this type of climate.
- It is found in the Amazon Basin in South America and in the Zaire basin in Africa.

3 Using graph **A**:
   a) What is the temperature for the equatorial climate in
   - January ● July?
   b) Why is it hot throughout the year?

4 **a)** Using graph **A**, how much rain falls in a year?
   b) Why do some places near to the Equator have snow lying all the year?

5 Describe three differences between an equatorial climate and Britain's climate.

Summary

Due to its latitude the equatorial climate is hot and wet throughout the year. The weather for one day is very similar to that of the next.

EQUATOR

What are tropical rainforests?

The **tropical rainforests** grow in the equatorial climate. They provide the most luxuriant vegetation found on earth. One third of the world's trees grow here. There are over 1,000 different types, including **hardwoods** such as mahogany, greenheart and rosewood. The vegetation has had to **adapt** to the climate. By adapt we mean that it has had to learn to live with the constant high temperatures and the heavy rainfall (diagram **A** and photo **B**).

A

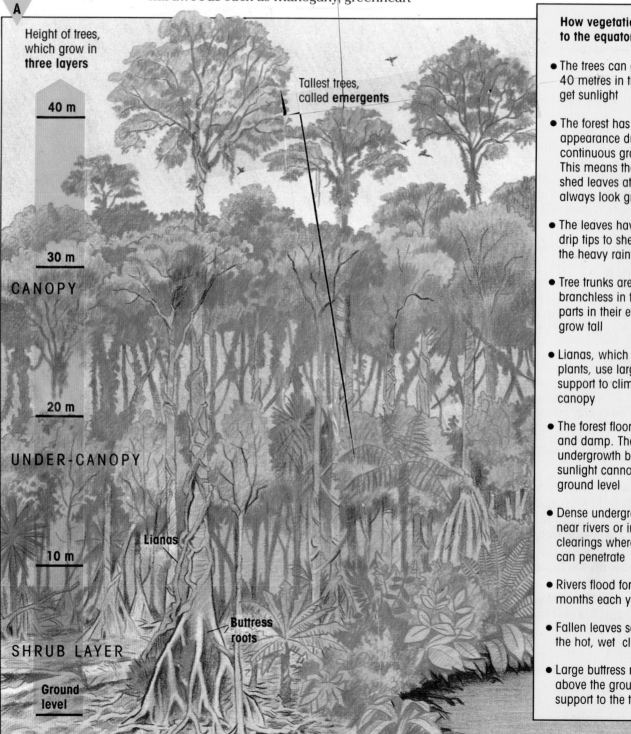

Height of trees, which grow in **three layers**

40 m

Tallest trees, called **emergents**

30 m

CANOPY

20 m

UNDER-CANOPY

10 m

Lianas

Buttress roots

SHRUB LAYER

Ground level

How vegetation has adapted to the equatorial climate

- The trees can grow to over 40 metres in the effort to get sunlight

- The forest has an **evergreen** appearance due to the continuous growing season. This means that trees can shed leaves at any time, but always look green and in leaf

- The leaves have drip tips to shed the heavy rainfall

- Tree trunks are straight and branchless in their lower parts in their efforts to grow tall

- Lianas, which are vine-like plants, use large trees as a support to climb up to the canopy

- The forest floor is dark and damp. There is little undergrowth because the sunlight cannot reach ground level

- Dense undergrowth develops near rivers or in forest clearings where sunlight can penetrate

- Rivers flood for several months each year

- Fallen leaves soon rot in the hot, wet climate

- Large buttress roots stand above the ground to give support to the trees

Most of the 1,000 types of trees have yet to be studied. Many may prove to be valuable to us. Over half of our known drugs (e.g. quinine which is used to treat malaria) have come from here. Recently one plant, a type of periwinkle, has been found to be successful in treating leukaemia in children. It is hoped that the rainforests may be a source of cures for other illnesses such as cancer and AIDS.

Wildlife

Apart from large animals which would find it difficult to move between the large trees, the rainforest is full of wildlife (diagram **C**). Some **species** live in the **canopy**; others live either in the **under-canopy**, on the forest floor or in the many swamps and rivers. Like the trees, wildlife has had to adapt in order to survive in this climate and vegetation.

B Tropical rainforest, Cameroon

A typical 10 kilometre square of rainforest might include:

- 750 species of tree
- 400 species of bird
- 150 species of butterfly
- 1,500 species of flowering plant
- 20 types of animal
- 100 types of reptile
- 60 types of amphibian
- countless numbers of insects and fish.

C

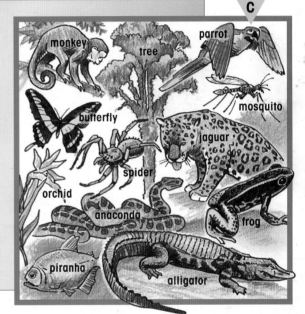

Activities

1 Match up each of the seven descriptive points of the tropical rainforest from the list below with its correct number from diagram **D**.

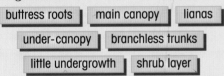

buttress roots	main canopy	lianas
under-canopy	branchless trunks
little undergrowth	shrub layer

Answer like this:

| 1 = Little undergrowth |

2 **a)** Why do trees grow so tall?
 b) Why are buttress roots needed?
 c) Why is there so little undergrowth?
 d) Why do plants grow so quickly?

D

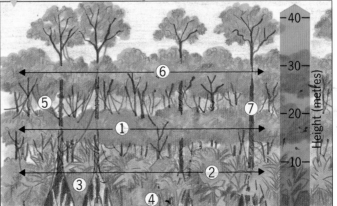

E X T R A

Describe how wildlife in the rainforest has had to adapt to living in the hot, wet, forest environment.

Summary   The tropical rainforests have more trees and wildlife than anywhere else on earth. All plants and wildlife have had to adapt to the hot and wet environment.

What is the climate of the hot deserts?

Graph **A** shows the **hot desert** type of climate. The highest temperatures on earth are recorded here, but they can fall rapidly in winter. Although deserts are very dry, most places do get some rain. However, amounts are small and unreliable.

How would you like our weather? Scorching hot in the day and freezing cold at night. We hardly ever see clouds or get rain. We get strong winds which cause sandstorms. The sand gets everywhere – in your eyes, ears, mouth and even up your nose!

A

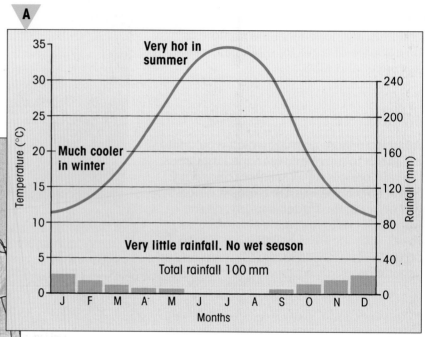

Very hot in summer

Much cooler in winter

Very little rainfall. No wet season

Total rainfall 100 mm

Temperature

In the hot deserts, unlike in Britain, there is a big difference between day and night-time temperatures. As the hot deserts rarely have any cloud the sun easily heats the ground during the day and temperatures can rise to 50°C. At night, with no cloud to keep in the heat, temperatures often fall near to freezing. Hot deserts have two seasons in a year. Summers are very hot while winters, although warm when compared to Britain, are much cooler.

The Sahara is the world's largest desert. Table **C** describes the factors affecting its temperature

Rainfall

Desert climates occur in places where air is **descending**. This is the opposite to Britain where the air usually **rises**. When air **rises** it cools and condenses to give cloud and rain. In deserts the **descending** air gets warmer, causes evaporation and gives cloudless skies. With few rivers and little vegetation the amount of water available for evaporation is limited.

C

	Why does the Sahara get hot summers?	Why are its winters much cooler?
Latitude	The sun is overhead at this time of year.	The sun is still high in the sky but is no longer overhead.
Distance from the sea	Land areas heat up rapidly. It is a long way from any cooling effect of the sea.	Land areas lose heat rapidly. It is a long way from any warming effect of the sea.
Prevailing wind	Blows from the warm land.	Blows from the cool land.

D

Why is the Sahara so dry?	
Prevailing wind	Blows from the land. No moisture to pick up and so too dry to form clouds or give rain.
Descending air	Air descends and warms up. As there is no condensation, skies remain cloudless and the weather stays dry.

Prevailing winds do not bring rain as they come from the land (table **D**). When the rain does fall it comes in heavy, convectional storms. Some places may get two or three storms in a single month and then go without rain for two or three years. That is why rainfall is said to be unreliable.

Which places have a hot desert climate?

Map **E** shows that this type of climate is found:
- In the centre or on the west coasts of continents.
- Usually between latitudes 10° and 30° north or south of the Equator.
- Where the prevailing wind comes from the dry land.

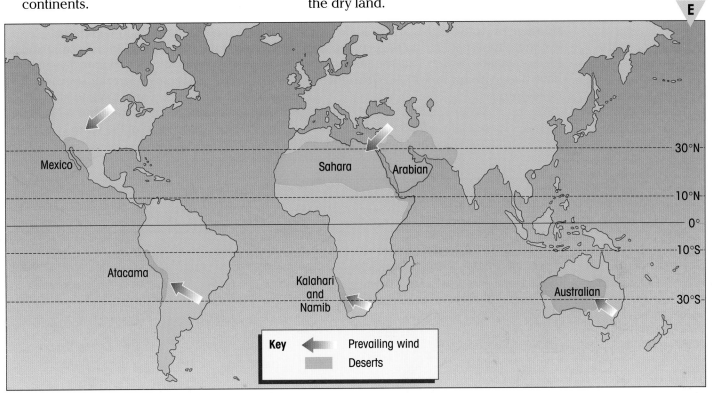

E

Mexico
Sahara
Arabian
30°N
10°N
0°
10°S
Atacama
Kalahari and Namib
Australian
30°S

Key — Prevailing wind
▬ Deserts

Activities

1 a) Name two hot deserts in Africa and two in the Americas.
   b) Give two reasons why they are found there.
   c) Give two points which describe the location of hot deserts.

2 Write out the paragraph below, choosing the correct word from the pair in brackets.

> The hot desert is very (cold/hot) in (summer/winter) and during the (day/night). It is much colder in (summer/winter) and during the (day/night). The amounts of cloud and rainfall are (large/small).

3 Diagram **F** explains why it rains a lot in Britain. Complete the diagram to explain why it does not rain very often in the hot deserts.

4 Using graph **A**:
   a) What is the temperature for the hot desert climate in:
   - January   - July?
   b) Give two reasons why it is so hot in summer and during the day.
   c) How much rain falls in a year?
   d) Give two reasons why deserts get so little rain.

F

| In Britain → air usually rises → air cools → condensation gives cloud and rain |

| In hot deserts → _____ → _____ → _____ and _____ |

Summary

The hot deserts are very hot during the day and in summer. They have cooler winters and cold nights. Clouds are few and rainfall is small in amount and is unreliable.

13

How do plants and wildlife survive in tropical deserts?

The biggest problem in the desert is the shortage of water. Plants and wildlife that live there have had to find ways of looking for, and storing, water. This means that they have had to **adapt** to living in **drought** conditions.

Only a few specially adapted plants can survive (diagram **A**). They have to grow a long way from neighbouring plants and they have to lie **dormant** for long periods. Dormant means that a plant is resting and is inactive (like most British plants during the winter). Occasional desert rainstorms will suddenly bring the plants back to life. Within hours the desert 'blooms' as each plant takes advantage of the extra water.

A

Saguaro cactus (photo **B**)
Takes 130 years to mature to a height of 15 metres. Can live for 200 years.

After heavy rain a large saguaro can soak up a thousand litres of water

It can store 8,000 litres of water

People lost in the desert have survived by cutting out part of the stem and drinking the moisture

Thorn bushes have no leaves

Arms usually grow only after 75 years

Spikes instead of leaves reduce loss of moisture and stop animals from eating the plant

Thick, waxy skin reflects some of the sun's heat and reduces loss of moisture

Cacti seeds can lie dormant for several years until it rains

Prickly pear cactus
Grows to full size (about 3 m high) in ten years

Yellow flowers

Fleshy stem to store water

Cacti have many long but shallow roots to soak up as much water as possible after rain

Some plants can store water in bulbs on their roots

B Saguaro cactus, Arizona, USA

C Prickly pear cactus in bloom, New Mexico, USA

D How the camel has adapted to desert conditions

Wildlife not only needs water but has to avoid the high daytime temperatures. Many species are **nocturnal** – they are only active at night. Some burrow into the sand to avoid the daytime heat. Others, like the camel, can store water (photo **D**). The gerenuk antelope never drinks but gets all its water from the plants upon which it feeds. Lizards are cold-blooded. They need heat to become active and then they can stand very high temperatures. Other wildlife includes insects such as scorpions, birds such as road-runners and sidewinder rattlesnakes.

Camels live in hot deserts and can store water for long journeys. They can close their eyes, nose and mouth in a sandstorm. They have large pads on their feet for walking over sand and stones. Their tough, leathery mouths let them eat the few thorny plants which grow in the desert.

Activities

1 **a)** Draw a large diagram of either a prickly pear cactus or a saguaro cactus. Put the following labels on your diagram:

  | fleshy stem | thick and waxy skin |

  | spiky leaves | long and shallow roots |

  b) Explain how each of the four labels listed in **a)** helps the cactus plant to search for, and to store, water.

2 Make a simple drawing of a camel. Label and describe the features which help it to live in hot desert conditions.

E X T R A

Write a list of instructions to a person who wishes to cross a desert. Your list might include advice on transport, clothing, food and drink.

Summary Desert plants and animals have to be able to search for, and store, water. They must also be able to survive the very hot days and very cold nights.

What is a Mediterranean climate?

A

Graph **B** shows the **Mediterranean** type of climate. It has two very different seasons. The weather in summer is hot and dry while in winter it is warm and wet.

B

[Climate graph showing temperature curve and rainfall bars over 12 months (J F M A M J J A S O N D). Temperature axis 0–30°C, Rainfall axis 0–240 mm. Labels: "Mild winters", "Very hot summers", "Total rainfall 400 mm", "Drought in summer", "Wet in winter".]

We like coming here in summer. It always seems to be hot, sunny and dry. Sometimes it can be too hot to sleep at night and you can get sunburnt in the day. We bet it is cold, wet and windy back in Britain.

Why are summers hot and dry?

Summers are hot because the sun rises high into the sky. Although it does not shine from directly overhead as it does nearer the Equator, it does rise higher than in places to the north, like Britain. The prevailing wind blows from the land (map **C**). As the land is hot at this time of year then the wind blowing from it will bring hot weather. As the land is also dry then the wind blowing over it cannot pick up much moisture. This means that most places have very little rain and several months of drought. Apart from an occasional thunderstorm most days are cloudless and sunny.

Why are winters warm and wet?

Although the sun is lower in the sky in winter it is still high enough to give warm days. The nearby sea, which was warmed during the summer, only loses its heat slowly in winter. This keeps places near to the coast warm. Frost and snow are unusual near sea-level. The prevailing wind blows from the opposite direction to that of summer (map **D**). As it now comes from the sea it brings air that is warm and moist. As the air rises over the many coastal mountains it gives large amounts of relief rainfall and, at higher altitudes, snow. However, wet days are usually separated by two or three days which are warm and sunny.

C

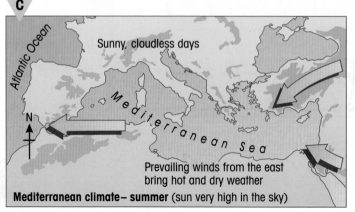

Mediterranean climate – **summer** (sun very high in the sky)

D

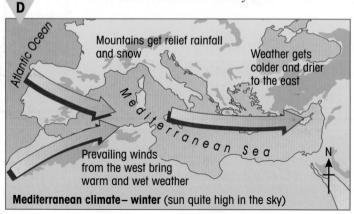

Mediterranean climate – **winter** (sun quite high in the sky)

Which places have a Mediterranean climate?

The name 'Mediterranean' is given to climates in several different parts of the world. Map **E** shows that this type of climate is usually found:

- on the west coasts of continents
- between latitudes 30° and 40° north and south of the Equator.

In summer the prevailing wind comes from the east and the weather is like that of the hot deserts (map **C**). In winter the prevailing wind comes from the west and the weather is more like ours in Britain (map **D**).

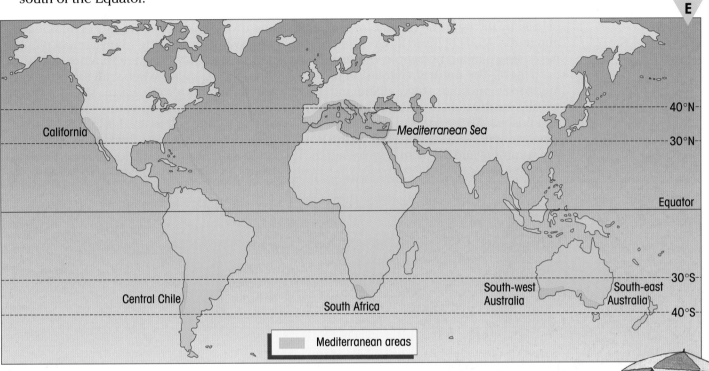

E

California
Mediterranean Sea — 40°N
30°N
Equator
Central Chile
South Africa
South-west Australia
South-east Australia
30°S
40°S

Mediterranean areas

Activities

1 Name the places in the world which have a Mediterranean type of climate.

2 **a)** Make a large copy of diagram **F**.
   b) Complete the sentences by adding the correct endings from the list in the box below:

   ...the prevailing wind blows from the land.
   ...the sun rises high in the sky.
   ...the warming effect of the sea.
   ...the prevailing wind blows from the sea.

3 **a)** What is the temperature for the Mediterranean climate in:
   - January
   - July?
   b) How much rain falls in an average year?

F

Hot summers because...   Mild winters because of...

Mediterranean climate

Dry summers because...   Wet winters because of...

E X T R A

Why does the Mediterranean type of climate attract:
   a) many British families for their summer holidays
   b) some elderly British people for most of the winter?

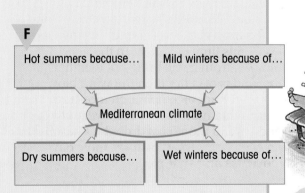

Summary

Places with a Mediterranean climate have hot, dry summers and warm, wet winters.

What is Mediterranean vegetation like?

Visitors to the Mediterranean in the spring and summer will see masses of brightly coloured flowers as they arrive by air or road. On reaching their destination they will be met by the perfume of numerous plants and herbs. Many of these flowers and herbs have been planted by people who have lived there. The **natural vegetation** of Mediterranean lands is woodland and **scrub**. Scrub refers to small, stunted trees and bushes. All the types of vegetation growing here have had to adapt to the hot, dry summers and the warm, wet winters (sketch **A**).

The growth of most Mediterranean plants begins with the start of the rainy season in autumn. Bulbs and scrub which have lain **dormant** (inactive) during the summer heat and drought put out new shoots and begin to flower. The seeds of many annual plants germinate. They continue to grow slowly through the winter when water is available and temperatures are warm. They flower in the spring when temperatures get warmer and while the soil is still damp. Seeds ripen in summer. They have thick coats as protection against the intense heat. Green plants, meanwhile, shrivel up to become stiff and thorny (sketch **A**). The evergreen trees grow slowly throughout the year.

A

Pine

Cypress

Cork oak

Some have thick bark as protection against the heat

Many have small, thin, waxy or leathery leaves to reduce moisture loss

WOODLAND

Thorn bush

LOW SCRUB

Sweet-smelling herbs

Rosemary

Lavender

Thyme

Very little grass – too hot and too dry

Quick life cycle to fit into the short growing season

Many plants have long roots to reach down to underground water

Rosemary can roll its leaves up tightly to reduce moisture loss

How has vegetation been changed by people?

Before people began to live around the Mediterranean Sea the land was covered in forest. Today very little is left and the main vegetation is scrub. This change can partly be blamed on a natural cause – a decline in rainfall. Mostly it is the result of activity by people who settled here, and their grazing animals. The trees were cut down for building houses and ships, and to be used as fuel. Young trees were eaten by herds of sheep and goats. Forest fires, some started deliberately, have added to the destruction. Some pine and cypress trees still grow in remote areas (photo **B**). Where the land is not used for farming or building it is either covered in a thick tangle of low, spiky shrubs or left as bare rock (photo **C**).

B Mediterranean woodland, Crete

C Mediterranean scrub, Crete

Activities

1 Name six Mediterranean plants.

2 **a)** Why do Mediterranean plants grow mainly in winter?
  b) Why do they only grow very slowly in summer?

3 Give three ways by which the Mediterranean vegetation can survive in the hot, dry summer.

4 Give three ways in which the natural Mediterranean vegetation has been altered by human activity.

5 The olive (diagram **D**) is an important tree and crop in many Mediterranean countries. Make a large copy of diagram **D** and complete it by adding the following labels:

| long roots | thick trunk | small leaves |

| fruit with a thick skin | thin soil |

D

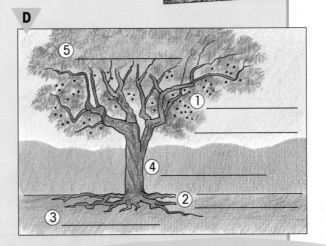

Summary Mediterranean vegetation has had to adapt to hot, dry summers and warm, wet winters. It has been affected by human activities such as the felling and burning of forests and the keeping of grazing animals.

19

What are volcanoes?

Volcanoes are openings (**vents**) in the ground where **magma** (molten rock) from deep inside the earth forces its way to the surface. The magma may appear as flows of molten **lava**, as **volcanic bombs**, as fragments of rock or simply as **ash** and **dust**. Mountains that are made of these materials are called volcanoes. Look at diagram **A**. It shows the main features of a volcano and gives an idea of what one looks like inside.

Volcanoes may be **active**, **dormant** or **extinct**.
- If a volcano has erupted recently and is likely to erupt again, it is described as active. There are over 700 active volcanoes around the world.

Mount Etna is an active volcano because it erupted as recently as 1971, 1983 and 1992 and is expected to erupt again in the near future.
- Volcanoes that have erupted in the past 2,000 years, but not recently, are said to be dormant or sleeping. These may be dangerous as it is difficult to predict when they are going to erupt again.
- Many volcanoes are unlikely ever to erupt again. They are said to be extinct because they are dead and their volcanic activity is finished. Britain's last volcanoes erupted over 50 million years ago and have mostly been worn away by erosion. The Edinburgh volcano in Scotland, and Snowdon in Wales, are examples of extinct volcanoes in Britain.

A

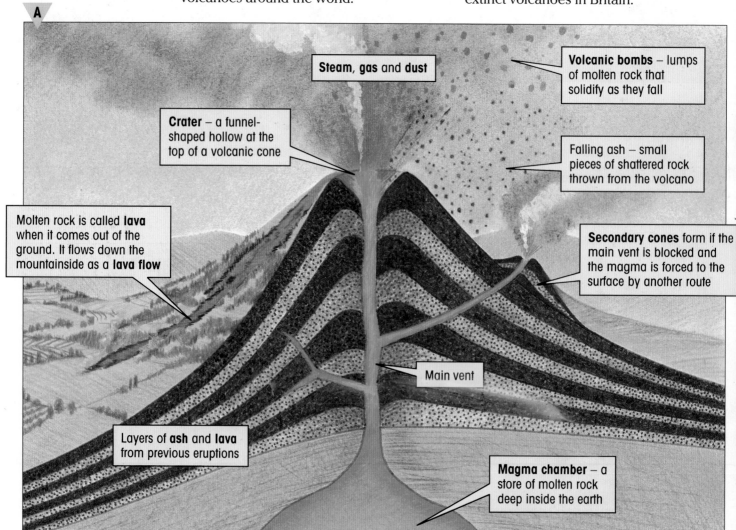

Steam, gas and **dust**

Volcanic bombs – lumps of molten rock that solidify as they fall

Crater – a funnel-shaped hollow at the top of a volcanic cone

Falling ash – small pieces of shattered rock thrown from the volcano

Molten rock is called **lava** when it comes out of the ground. It flows down the mountainside as a **lava flow**

Secondary cones form if the main vent is blocked and the magma is forced to the surface by another route

Main vent

Layers of **ash** and **lava** from previous eruptions

Magma chamber – a store of molten rock deep inside the earth

When a volcano erupts, the magma from below the earth's surface rises up the vent to the volcano's crater. It then explodes into the air as ash, dust and volcanic bombs, or flows out as molten lava.

Some eruptions are spectacular and take the form of huge and violent explosions. The greatest volcanic explosion of modern times happened when the Indonesian island of Krakatoa erupted in 1883. The noise from that was so loud that it could be heard over 4,700 km (3,000 miles) away in Australia – see map **A** on page 26.

Not all eruptions are like Krakatoa. Some can be quite gentle and fairly peaceful. Mauna Loa on Hawaii, for example, pours out a steady stream of liquid lava with only a small amount of explosive force and occasional danger to nearby settlements.

Most volcanoes are cone-shaped but the steepness of their slopes can vary considerably. This steepness depends mainly on the type of lava erupted from the vent. Some different types of volcano are shown in diagrams **B**, **C** and **D**.

B

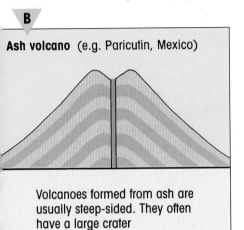

Ash volcano (e.g. Paricutin, Mexico)

Volcanoes formed from ash are usually steep-sided. They often have a large crater

C

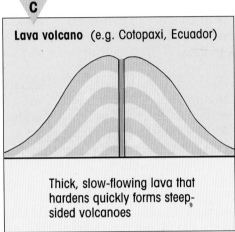

Lava volcano (e.g. Cotopaxi, Ecuador)

Thick, slow-flowing lava that hardens quickly forms steep-sided volcanoes

D

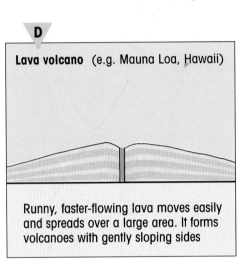

Lava volcano (e.g. Mauna Loa, Hawaii)

Runny, faster-flowing lava moves easily and spreads over a large area. It forms volcanoes with gently sloping sides

Activities

1 **a)** What are volcanoes?
   b) What is the difference between active, dormant and extinct volcanoes?

2 Give the meaning of the words below. You could add sketches to some of them to make them clearer and more interesting.

   | magma | vent | crater | lava |

   | volcanic bombs | volcanic cone |

3 Make a simple sketch of photo **E** and label the following:

   | two craters | steam coming out of vent |

   | volcanic cone | ash and lava |

   Give your sketch a title.

4 Make a large drawing of a volcano like the one in sketch **A**. Label the features shown in bold type. Underneath your sketch write a description to explain what happens when it erupts. Try to mention all the labelled features.

E Crater of Ngauruhoe, New Zealand

Summary

Volcanoes are cone-shaped mountains made from magma that has come from deep below the ground.

What happens when a volcano erupts?

When a volcano erupts it can cause serious problems. People are put in danger and their surroundings can be severely damaged. Problems like this are called **natural hazards**. Earthquakes, floods, drought and strong winds are also examples of natural hazards. In spite of the danger and possibility of great destruction, a lot of people often live in volcanic areas. This is because ash and lava turn into rich fertile soil which is good for farming. Good farming areas are attractive places to live.

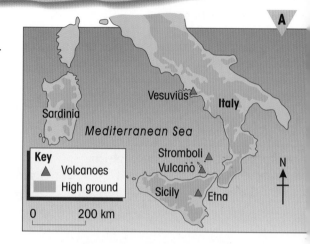

The largest and most active volcano in Europe is the 3,340 metre high Mount Etna. This volcano is located on the Italian island of Sicily and it continuously rumbles and steams. Several times this century Etna has had major eruptions when masses of ash, volcanic bombs and lava have been blasted out of the cone, destroying the surrounding area. Over a million people live in the Mount Etna area and these eruptions have caused considerable problems for them.

Mount Etna erupted most recently in 1971, 1983 and 1992. In 1971 the eruption began with a huge explosion that sounded like a jet aircraft taking off. This was followed by a spectacular fireworks display when red hot ash was thrown hundreds of metres into the air and molten lava poured down the mountainside. In this eruption most of the ski slopes and cable car stations were destroyed and a research observatory near the summit was completely wiped out.

The 'fireworks display' eruption of Mount Etna in 1971

The 1983 eruption began in March and continued for several months. Millions of tonnes of lava gushed out of the crater and engulfed a hotel, three restaurants, 25 houses and numerous orange groves and vineyards. The lava flowed at an average speed of 15 km per hour (about the speed you ride a bicycle) and at one time threatened to bury several small villages in its path. Eventually a diversion was made and after a series of controlled explosions, the lava was diverted and the villages saved.

C Damage caused by the lava flows of the 1983 eruption of Mount Etna

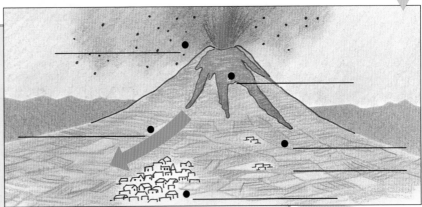

D

Activities

1 Why do volcanic areas often have a lot of people living in them?

2 **a)** What is meant by the term 'natural hazard'?
   b) Give four examples of natural hazards.

3 Describe what happens when Mount Etna erupts by sorting the boxes below into the correct order. Link your boxes with arrows and add a title. You might like to make simple drawings for each box to make your description clearer and more interesting.

Lava pours down the mountainside	Buildings and property damaged
Rescue service goes into action	Volcano gently rumbles and steams
Loud explosion as volcano erupts	Ash, bombs and lava blasted out of volcano

4 **a)** Make a simple copy of sketch **D** and put the following labels in the correct places.

| lava flows | threatened settlement |
| diversion channel | ash and bombs |
| vineyards and orange groves |

b) Underneath your sketch list eight problems caused by Mount Etna erupting.

Summary

When volcanoes like Mount Etna erupt they may bring danger to people and cause severe damage to property and the surroundings. Disasters caused by great forces such as volcanic eruptions, earthquakes, floods and strong winds are called natural hazards.

What happens in an earthquake?

On Tuesday 17 October 1989 an **earthquake** hit the Californian city of San Francisco. These two pages explain through photos and newspaper articles what happened on that day.

A

Key
- Built-up area
- Rural area

0   10   20 km

Area of main map

Bay Bridge

Golden Gate Bridge

Oakland

San Francisco

Fires in Marina district

Candlestick Park closed

San Francisco airport closed

Section of bridge collapses

Upper deck of Nimitz Highway collapses

N

Shock waves

Epicentre of earthquake

Pacific Ocean

B

Quake hits 'Frisco'

At least 63 people were killed and over 3,000 were injured when an earthquake struck San Francisco at 5.04 p.m. yesterday. It ripped 10ft cracks in roads and a packed highway collapsed, crushing 253 motorists. Rescue workers struggled to free people from damaged buildings while fires roared throughout the city. More than a million homes were plunged into darkness and over 13,000 people were made homeless. Eyewitnesses said they heard a low rumbling noise before the quake hit. Everything then began to shake and buildings started to fall apart. Estimates of the damage already stand at $7 billion. President Bush has promised immediate aid.

(Wednesday 18 October, *San Francisco Herald*)

C

'The whole world was shaking'

At San Francisco's City Hall, terrified staff dived under desks as pieces of the ceiling and walls came down. Across the street in the health department a giant gusher of water shot through the second floor.

Near the tourist area of Fisherman's Wharf an entire four-storey apartment block collapsed. A woman from the third floor said, 'It seemed like the whole world was shaking. I ran to the stairs to escape but they had gone. There was just a hole. I had to use the fire escape.' Others were not so lucky. They were trapped and couldn't get out.

Fires were inevitable. In one of the worst, a broken gas main exploded turning an entire block in the Marina district into a raging inferno. Firemen were unable to control the blaze which roared on through the night.

(Thursday 19 October, *Daily Mail*)

D

Big shake wrecks road

An estimated 200 people were killed when a mile of two-tier road known as the Nimitz Highway collapsed. The road was built to be earthquake proof but the 'big shake' was too much for it. A huge section collapsed onto the road below, squashing hundreds of cars into a space that in places was just 12 inches high.

Further along the highway on the Bay Bridge, more motorists were killed when part of the bridge collapsed. A woman driver on the bridge at the time said, 'The whole structure wobbled and a great gap appeared in the roadway. Cars skidded out of control and some toppled over the edge'.

At Candlestick Park 60,000 baseball fans were packed into the stadium for the game between the Giants and the Athletics. The game had just begun when the earth began to shake and violent tremors ran through the stadium. Cracks opened up in the concrete stands and ripples over a foot high ran right across the park.

Several people were hit by chunks of falling metal and concrete but no-one was killed.

(Thursday 19 October, *The Californian*)

Activities

1 Complete an earthquake fact file using these headings.

E ▼   Fact file

Place _____	Injured _____
Date _____	Homeless _____
Time _____	Damage cost _____
Dead _____	

2 Look at the headlines below about the San Francisco earthquake. Write a newsflash to be read out on television giving news about the earthquake. Write about 40 words on each of any four of the headlines given below.

F ▼

Baseball blitzed   Many trapped

Buildings toppled   Fires rage

Bridge collapses   Highway squashed

E X T R A

Below is a list of problems that faced the authorities after the earthquake. Which four do you consider to be the most urgent? Give reasons for your choice.

- Provide new homes for people
- Search for missing people
- Supply medicine
- Rescue stranded people
- Evacuate people in danger
- Supply food
- Supply drinking water

Summary

Earthquakes make the ground shake and may cause buildings and other structures to collapse. Some earthquakes are violent and may cause severe hazards for people.

Where do volcanoes and earthquakes happen?

There are thousands of volcanoes around the world. Some are extinct, some are dormant and some may be erupting even as you read this book. When they do erupt you can be sure that wherever they are, there will be danger and probable damage.

Scientists now know a lot about volcanoes but they still find it difficult to predict exactly where and when an eruption will actually happen. What we do know, however, is that volcanic eruptions do not occur just anywhere on the earth's surface but they are confined to certain areas. Map **A** shows these areas.

Notice that most volcanoes occur in narrow belts or are grouped together in small clumps. One belt runs all the way round the edge of the Pacific Ocean and is called the '**Ring of Fire**'. Another belt runs through the islands of the Indian Ocean. There is also great volcanic activity on Iceland. Can you find the area in the Mediterranean Sea where the volcanoes of Italy are located?

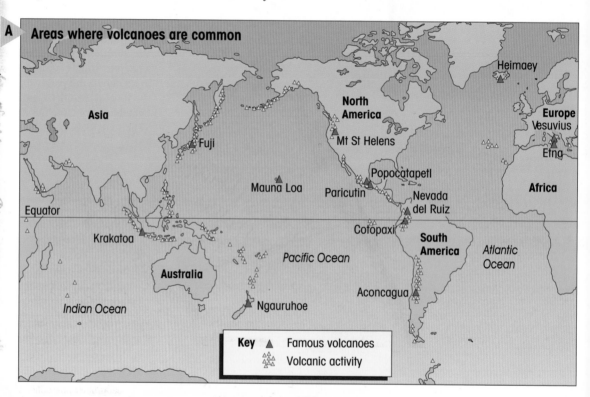

A Areas where volcanoes are common

Key ▲ Famous volcanoes
△ Volcanic activity

Heimaey · North America · Asia · Europe · Vesuvius · Fuji · Mt St Helens · Etna · Popocatapetl · Mauna Loa · Paricutin · Nevada del Ruiz · Africa · Equator · Cotopaxi · South America · Krakatoa · Pacific Ocean · Atlantic Ocean · Australia · Aconcagua · Indian Ocean · Ngauruhoe

Activities

1 **a)** Which four of the following describe where volcanoes may be found?
- All over the world
- In narrow belts
- In Iceland
- In Japan
- In Central Asia
- Along the west coast of North and
- South America
- In Australia

b) Name two other places where volcanoes may be found.

2 Suggest reasons for the name of 'Ring of Fire'.

3 You may need an atlas for this question. Match each of the volcanoes named on map **A** with a country from the list in the box below. Some countries may be used more than once.

New Zealand • Colombia • Japan • Mexico • Italy • Argentina • Indonesia • Iceland • Ecuador • USA

Earthquakes are happening all the time. Some are so weak that they can hardly be felt and instruments called **seismographs** are needed to detect them. Others, like the San Francisco earthquake, are so powerful that the shaking of the ground causes buildings to collapse and landslides to occur.

Earthquakes can occur anywhere, but they are much more common in some places than in others. Map **B** shows where earthquakes regularly happen. Look carefully at their distribution. They are mostly arranged in long narrow belts. One belt goes down the middle of the Atlantic Ocean. Another follows the west coast of North and South America and then goes all the way round the edge of the Pacific Ocean to New Zealand. Try to identify some other belts.

Now compare map **B**, showing earthquakes, with map **A**, showing volcanoes. Notice how similar they are. Look particulary at the 'Ring of Fire' and the Mediterranean countries. From studying maps like these, scientists have concluded that volcanoes and earthquakes often occur in the same places and are usually found in long narrow **zones of activity**. These areas can be the most dangerous places on ea°**⌐**

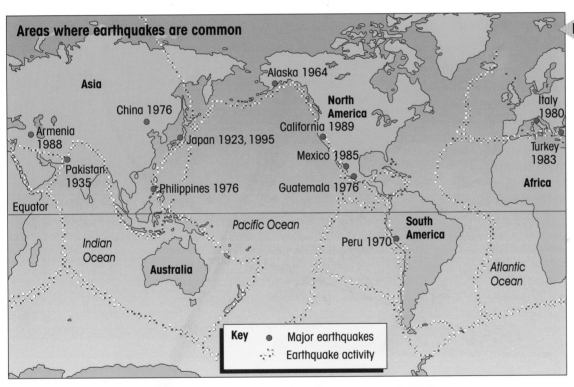

Areas where earthquakes are common

B

Alaska 1964

Asia

China 1976

North America

Italy 1980

Armenia 1988

California 1989

Japan 1923, 1995

Turkey 1983

Pakistan 1935

Mexico 1985

Africa

Philippines 1976

Guatemala 1976

Equator

Pacific Ocean

South America

Indian Ocean

Peru 1970

Australia

Atlantic Ocean

Key • Major earthquakes
‑∙‑∙ Earthquake activity

E X T R A

geography interactions 27B

4 Use the information on this page to describe where earthquakes happen.

5 Name five places where a scientist could study both volcanoes **and** earthquakes in the same area.

6 The eastern part of South America is an area largely without volcanoes and earthquakes. Name five other land areas where volcanic eruptions and earthquakes are uncommon.

Use books from home or the library to find out more about one of the volcanoes or earthquakes on map **A** or map **B**.

Write a short project about it. Try to include:
■ a map to show its location
■ a description of the eruption or earthquake
■ a list of damage it caused
■ labelled drawings to show what happened.

Summary

Most volcanoes and earthquakes are found in long narrow belts across the earth's surface. The main zones of activity lie along the west coast of the Americas and among islands of the Pacific and Indian Oceans.

How do volcanoes and earthquakes happen?

As you have seen on pages 26 and 27, volcanoes and earthquakes often occur in the same places and are usually found in long narrow belts. This gives a clue about how they happen.

The earth was formed 4,600 million years ago. Since then it has been slowly cooling down and a thin **crust** has formed round the outside. The crust is not all one piece but is broken into several enormous sections called **plates**. Some of the plates are as large as continents while others are much smaller. Underneath the crust the rock is so hot that it remains molten and can flow like treacle. The plates float on this layer and move about very, very slowly – just a few millimetres a year. In some places they move towards each other and in others they move apart or scrape alongside each other. The place where two plates meet is called a **plate boundary** (diagram **A**). The movement at these plate boundaries can cause earthquakes and volcanic eruptions to occur.

Look at map **B** which shows the major plate boundaries. Compare it with the volcanoes map on page 26 and the earthquakes map on page 27. Look

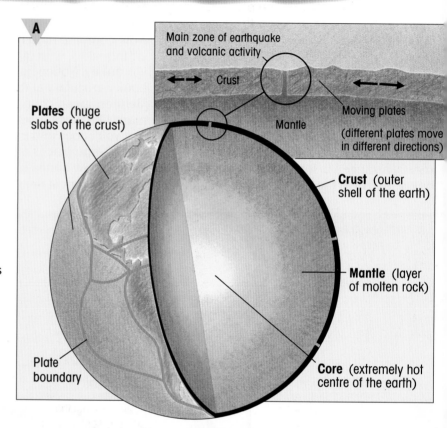

particularly at the 'Ring of Fire' around the Pacific Ocean. You should be able to see that most of the volcanoes and earthquakes happen along the plate boundaries.

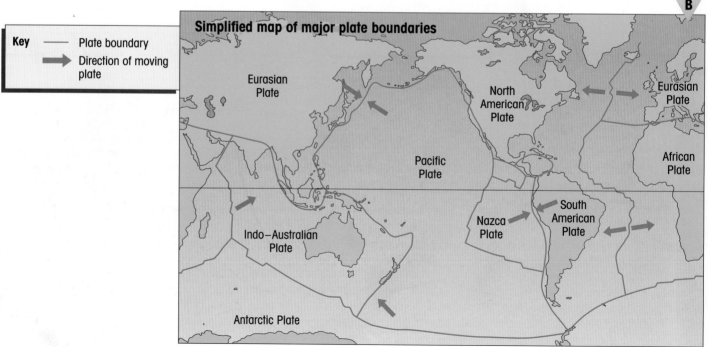

28

Diagram **C** shows what happens where plates move together. Here, on the west coast of South America, the Nazca Plate is being forced towards and underneath the South American Plate. As the plates move together the friction between them makes the rock melt. The liquid rock (magma) rises upwards and erupts on the surface as a volcano. The movement of the plates scraping together also makes the ground shake and sets off earthquakes. South America has over a hundred volcanoes caused in this way and in some places earthquakes happen every day.

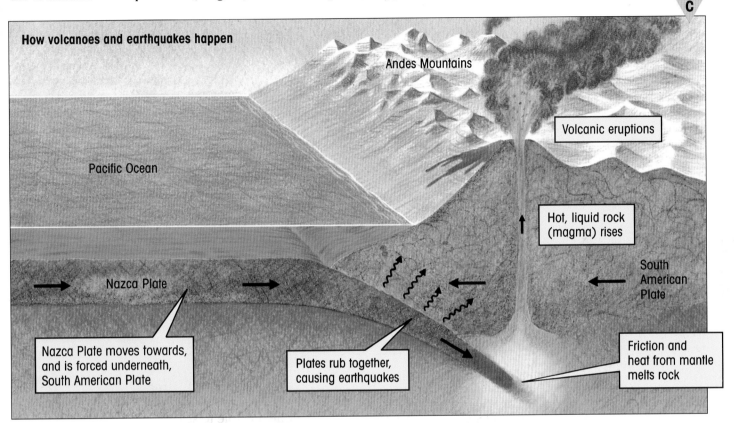

How volcanoes and earthquakes happen

Andes Mountains

Volcanic eruptions

Pacific Ocean

Hot, liquid rock (magma) rises

South American Plate

Nazca Plate

Nazca Plate moves towards, and is forced underneath, South American Plate

Plates rub together, causing earthquakes

Friction and heat from mantle melts rock

C

Activities

1 Look carefully at map **B**.
   a) On which plate does Britain lie?
   b) Why does Britain have no active volcanoes or major earthquakes?
   c) Which two plates meet along the west coast of the USA?
   d) Why do earthquakes happen in San Francisco?

2 Sort the statements below into the correct order to show how volcanoes can happen at plate boundaries.
   ● Molten rock rises
   ● Friction melts the rock
   ● Plates rub together
   ● Volcanoes erupt on the surface
   ● Plates move towards each other

3 How does the movement of plates cause earthquakes?

4 a) Make a larger copy of cross-section **D**.
   b) Name the two plates, the Andes mountains and the Pacific Ocean.
   c) Draw arrows to show plate movements.
   d) Put a circle round the zone of activity where there is friction, earthquakes and melting of rock.
   e) Add a title.

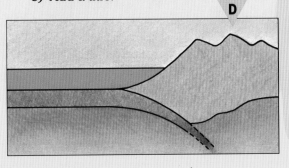

D

Summary

The earth's surface is made up of several plates that move about very slowly. Volcanoes and earthquakes are most likely to occur in areas where the plates meet.

What is soil?

Soil is dirty and gets on to your hands, clothes and shoes

Soil is essential for plants and crops to grow. Without soil there would be no animal or human life.

Soil is a thin layer that lies on the earth's surface. It is usually less than one metre in depth. It takes a long time for soil to form – often over 1,000 years to produce 1 cm. It is a vital natural resource which must be used carefully or it will become useless.

There are many different types of soil. Each soil depends upon the climate of a place, the vegetation which grows there and the type of underlying rock. In many places the natural soil has been altered by human activities such as farming and forestry. In some cases this has caused problems for people.

Photo **A** shows a section through a soil in northern Britain. You can see the vegetation at the top. The soil in this photo has two distinct layers.

How do soils differ?

Soils differ in several ways. Four of these differences are **texture**, **depth**, **colour** and **organic content**. It is quite easy to find these differences for yourself just by looking at, measuring and feeling a soil.

A Soil profile

Texture is how a soil feels when you touch it. This can easily be done by picking up some soil and trying to roll it into a ball. Diagram **B** explains some different textures. Depth, organic content and colour are explained in diagram **C**.

B

My soil feels gritty and it does not stick together.

My soil is mainly **sand**

My soil feels smooth - rather like soap. It sticks together quite well.

My soil is mainly **silt**

My soil easily rolls into a ball. It sticks together and to my fingers.

My soil is mainly **clay**

Depth
This is found by measuring the distance between the ground surface and the top of the underlying rock.

Organic content
The remains of dead leaves, roots, plants and animals can often be seen in the soil. These rot away to form **humus**. Humus is rich in goodness which helps plants and crops to grow.

Colour
Humus also affects the colour of a soil. To record the colour, first rub your fingers into the soil then rub the soil onto white paper. No soil will have all the colours shown above.

Collect your own soil samples from at least two different sites and study them. Record your results in a table like that shown in table **E**. Remember to replace the soil and vegetation when you have finished.

Activities

1 a) What is soil?
   b) Why is soil so important to us?

2 Most plants and crops need at least 40 cm of soil to grow in. How long might it take for that depth of soil to form?

3 Diagram **D** shows two different soils. Look at them and then copy out and complete table **E** below.

E

	Soil X	Soil Y
Texture		
Soil depth		
Organic content a) amount b) type		
Colour a) near top b) near bottom		

EXTRA

Summary

Soil is a vital resource which we cannot do without. It takes a long time for soil to form, so care has to be taken not to damage or destroy it in any way. Soils show differences in texture, depth, organic content and colour.

31

What is soil erosion?

Soil is one of our most important resources. We depend on it for most of the food that we eat and without it we would be unable to survive. Yet each year some 75 million tonnes of soil are lost around the world. The removal of soil from one place and its deposition elsewhere is called **soil erosion**.

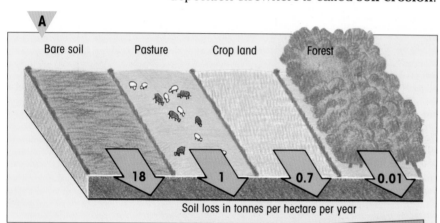

A

Bare soil   Pasture   Crop land   Forest

18   1   0.7   0.01

Soil loss in tonnes per hectare per year

B

Overgrazing by camels in Sudan

Soil is usually blown away by the wind or washed away by water running over the ground's surface. Erosion is greatest on steep slopes and when the soil is bare. It is least when there is a thick cover of vegetation. This is because plants and trees provide shelter from rain and wind and their root systems hold together the soil particles, making them difficult to remove. Diagram **A** shows how different types of ground cover are affected by soil erosion in eastern England.

Soil erosion is a natural process but in some places it has been increased by bad farming methods.

● **Overgrazing**
Sometimes too many animals are kept in one area. They eat all the vegetation and it dies off. This leaves the ground bare and unprotected as in photo **B**. Wind and rain can then carry off the loose soil.

● **Up and down ploughing**
Farmers find it easier to plough up and down a slope rather than across it. When it rains, water flows straight down the furrows and takes with it large amounts of soil. The furrows can quickly turn into deep gullies like those in photo **C**.

● **Deforestation**
This is the clearing away of forests, usually so that the land can be used for growing crops. Once the trees have gone there are no leaves to protect the soil from rainfall and no roots to hold the soil in place. This makes it easy for the soil to be washed or blown away.

● **Soil exhaustion**
Sometimes the soil is overused by the growing of too many crops. Eventually it loses its goodness, crops can no longer grow and the bare soil is quickly removed by the action of wind and water.

C Soil erosion

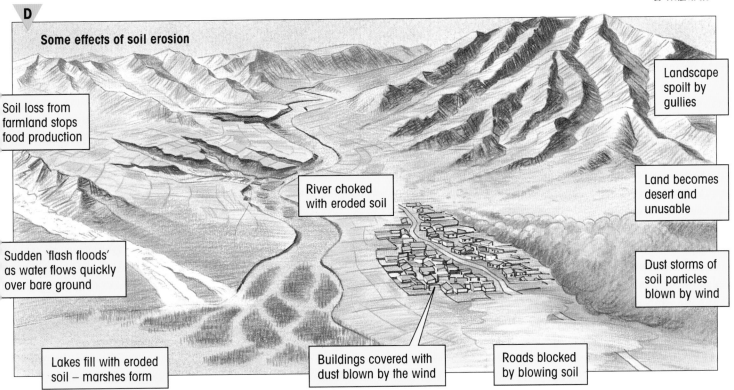

D Some effects of soil erosion

Soil loss from farmland stops food production

Landscape spoilt by gullies

River choked with eroded soil

Land becomes desert and unusable

Sudden 'flash floods' as water flows quickly over bare ground

Dust storms of soil particles blown by wind

Lakes fill with eroded soil – marshes form

Buildings covered with dust blown by the wind

Roads blocked by blowing soil

Activities

1 Why is soil so important to us?

2 Draw a tree and label it to show how it can help prevent soil erosion.

3 Describe how each of the farming methods shown in diagram **E** can cause soil erosion. You could add drawings for each one to make your descriptions clearer.

4 Copy table **F** below and complete it by writing the effects of soil erosion in the correct columns. Write no more than six words for each effect. Some effects may go in both columns. Give your table a title.

During a period of drought and wind	After a day of heavy rain

E

EXTRA

Imagine you are head of the village shown in diagram **D**. Write a letter to the farmer in the area whose methods are causing soil erosion. Explain the effects that his methods are having and suggest how they might be reduced.

Summary

Soil erosion is the removal of soil by wind or water. Where leaves intercept the rainfall and roots bind the soil together, erosion is slow. Where people and animals have removed the vegetation cover, soil erosion can be a serious problem.

Soil erosion in Nepal

For some countries soil erosion is a major hazard. It may not be spectacular like volcanic eruptions or earthquakes but it can still cause problems for people and damage to the environment. The mountain kingdom of Nepal is an example of a country that is badly affected by soil erosion.

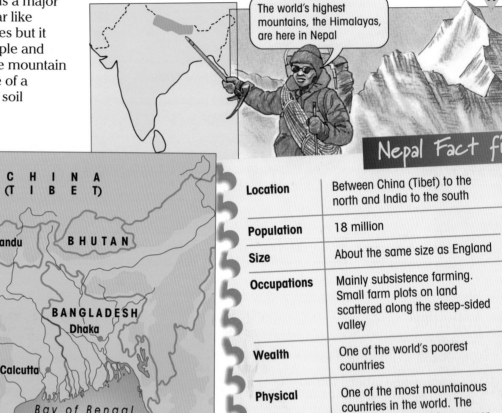

The world's highest mountains, the Himalayas, are here in Nepal

A

B

Key
- Highland
- Lowland
- • Main cities
- — Boundary

Nepal Fact file

Location	Between China (Tibet) to the north and India to the south
Population	18 million
Size	About the same size as England
Occupations	Mainly subsistence farming. Small farm plots on land scattered along the steep-sided valley
Wealth	One of the world's poorest countries
Physical	One of the most mountainous countries in the world. The climate is very wet in summer and very dry in winter.

Soil erosion has always been a problem in Nepal because of melting snow, heavy rain, unstable soil and steep slopes. Recently, however, the problem has become worse. Nepal's population has doubled in the last 30 years and tourism has increased considerably. This has led to changes in land use and management which in some cases have been damaging to the environment. In the worst cases whole hillsides have been cleared of trees to provide firewood and additional farmland for the extra people. Severe soil erosion has quickly followed as the bare unprotected soil has been washed away by the heavy summer rain.

The increase in erosion has not only affected Nepal but has also caused problems for nearby India and Bangladesh. Due mainly to deforestation the amount of water in the streams and rivers has increased dramatically. This has caused flooding in many places with a loss of farmland, breakdown of communication links and already the deaths of thousands of people.

C Soil erosion in Nepal

D The erosion problem in Nepal

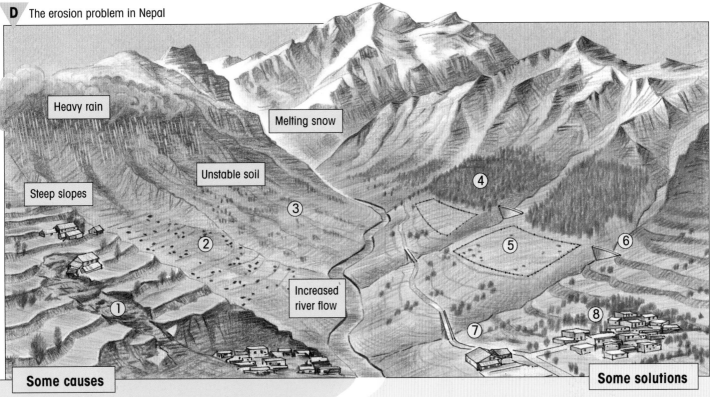

Labels on the image: Heavy rain, Melting snow, Unstable soil, Steep slopes, Increased river flow

Some causes

① **Collapsed terracing** Farming is only made possible by terracing the valley sides. On steep slopes the terracing may collapse in heavy rain.

② **Overgrazing** In Nepal animals are important for transport, ploughing and food. With the increase in population farmers began keeping too many animals. These have killed off the vegetation, leaving the ground bare.

③ **Deforestation** One third of Nepal's forest has been lost in the last ten years. Most has been cut down for firewood by the increasing population. Tourists (trekkers) each use more firewood per day than locals use in a week.

Some solutions

④ **Tree planting programme**, started by the Nepalese government, to cover bare slopes and reduce run-off

⑤ **Fenced areas** for grazing of fewer animals

⑥ **Small dams** built across gullies to control water flow

⑦ **Government agencies** set up in the valleys to encourage farmers to protect their remaining soil

⑧ **Self-help schemes** for villagers to plant and care for new trees in their own locality

Activities

1 What are the causes of soil erosion in Nepal? List your answers under the headings:
   - Natural processes
   - Human activities.

2 Suggest solutions to any two causes of soil erosion in Nepal brought about by changes in land management.

3 Explain the two newspaper headlines below. Write about 50 words for each one.

Nepal blames tourists for erosion

Bangladesh blames Nepal for floods

EXTRA

- Draw a map to show Nepal, India and Bangladesh.
- Mark the Himalayas and the main rivers.
- Name the cities of Kathmandu, Dhaka, Calcutta and Patna.
- Shade in **brown** the areas where soil erosion will be greatest.
- Shade in **green** where deposition and flooding will be most likely.

Summary

Soil erosion in Nepal is a result of both natural processes and the way people use the land. Careful management of the land can help reduce the problem of erosion.

How does global warming affect us?

The world is now warmer than it has been for many thousands of years. Some scientists believe that in future it will get even hotter. This is called **global warming** and may cause serious problems on our planet.

Global warming is thought to be due to the **greenhouse effect**. The earth is surrounded by a layer of gases including carbon dioxide. These keep the earth warm by preventing the escape of heat that would normally be lost from the atmosphere. The gases act rather like the glass in a greenhouse. They let heat in but prevent most of it from getting out.

The burning of **fossil fuels** such as oil, natural gas and coal produce large amounts of carbon dioxide. As the amount of this gas increases, the earth becomes warmer. Some people think that over the next 100 years temperatures may rise by 2–3°C. Others are not so certain and believe that other effects might cancel out this warming and may even produce colder conditions. Whoever is right, it is fairly certain that in the years ahead it is unlikely that conditions on earth will be the same as they are now.

Nobody knows exactly what the effects of global warming will be. Some of the things that scientists expect might happen are as follows.

- Polar ice caps and glaciers would start to melt as temperatures increased.
- Melting ice would cause the sea level to rise.
- Low lying areas would be flooded.
- More violent storms and extreme weather might occur.
- Hot regions would become hotter and deserts would spread.
- Climatic belts and vegetation types would move.
- Some plants and animals would become extinct.
- Heating and energy bills could be reduced.

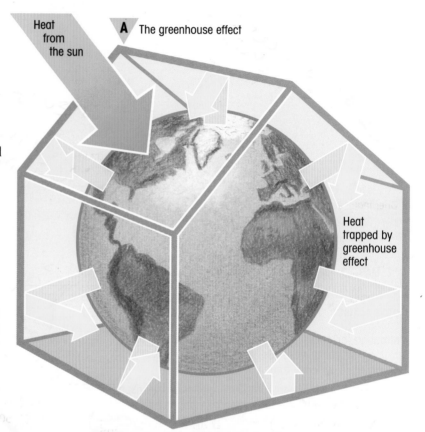

A The greenhouse effect

Heat from the sun

Heat trapped by greenhouse effect

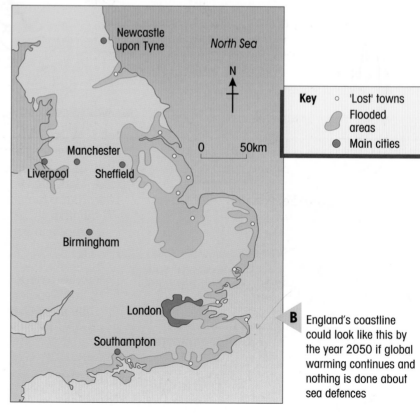

North Sea

N

Key
- ○ 'Lost' towns
- Flooded areas
- ● Main cities

0   50km

Newcastle upon Tyne

Manchester
Liverpool   Sheffield

Birmingham

London

Southampton

B England's coastline could look like this by the year 2050 if global warming continues and nothing is done about sea defences

C Some of the things that would happen by the year 2050 if global warming continues at its present rate

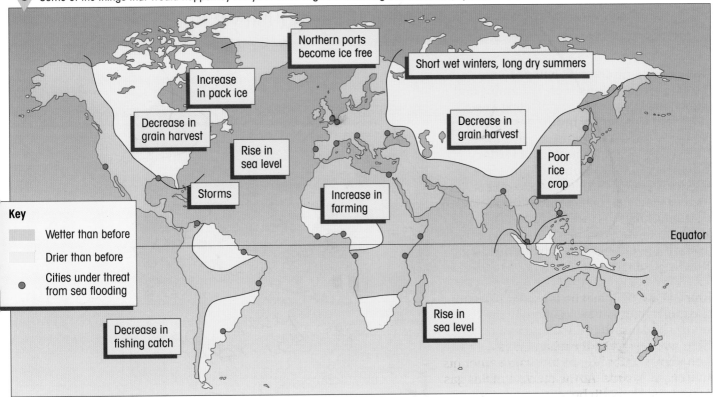

Northern ports become ice free

Increase in pack ice

Short wet winters, long dry summers

Decrease in grain harvest

Decrease in grain harvest

Rise in sea level

Poor rice crop

Storms

Increase in farming

Equator

Key
- Wetter than before
- Drier than before
- ● Cities under threat from sea flooding

Rise in sea level

Decrease in fishing catch

Activities

1 **a)** Make a larger copy of graph **D** and complete it using the figures given.
   b) Is the increase in carbon dioxide a steady one or is it getting faster?
   c) Describe why the level of carbon dioxide in the atmosphere is increasing.

2 **a)** What is global warming?
   b) Use words and diagrams to explain how the burning of fossil fuels may cause global warming.

3 Give three **good** effects and three **bad** effects of global warming.

4 You may need to use an atlas for this question.
   a) Name two cities from each continent that may be under threat from flooding.
   b) Name three countries where conditions may become drier than before.
   c) Name England's 'lost' towns from map **B**.

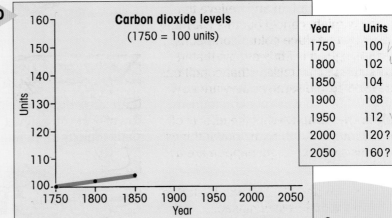

D

Carbon dioxide levels
(1750 = 100 units)

Year	Units
1750	100
1800	102
1850	104
1900	108
1950	112
2000	120?
2050	160?

5 List the things that might happen to Britain because of global warming.

E X T R A

Write a letter to your MP describing the problem of global warming and suggesting what could be done to reduce it. Write about 150 words.

Summary

The burning of fossil fuels has led to an increase in carbon dioxide in the atmosphere and a raising of the earth's temperature. A rise in sea level and a shift in the world climatic belts are two possible outcomes of global warming.

What is the tourist industry?

There are many different types of jobs. **Primary occupations** such as farming and mining involve people in collecting raw materials. **Secondary industries** employ people to make things, usually in a factory. A third type of employment is in **tertiary industries**. Tertiary industries provide a **service**. People who give help to others such as teachers, nurses and shop assistants are part of this industry. The number of jobs available in the tertiary sector is increasing. This is partly due to the growth of tourism.

Tourists are people who travel for pleasure. The tourist industry looks after the needs of tourists and provides the things that help them get to places to relax and enjoy themselves. The industry employs a large number of people. Travel agents, hotel waiters, tour guides and other such people rely on tourism for their livelihood. Sketch **B** shows some occupations in the tourist industry. Can you think of any more?

Tourism is big business. It is one of the world's fastest growing industries and by the year 2000 is expected to employ more people worldwide than any other industry. In 1990, £10.4 billion was spent on tourism in Britain alone. Graph **A** shows the increase in tourist numbers worldwide.

A

Millions of tourists

Year	Millions
1960	70
'65	75
'70	150
'75	210
'80	280
'85	320
'90	350
'95	370
2000	?

There are no signs of this increase slowing down. Can you estimate from the graph how many tourists there may be by the year 2000?

B

Airline pilot · Travel agent · Hotel manager · Ski instructor · Restaurant owner · Coach driver · Chef · Souvenir seller · Entertainer · Ferry operator · Tour guide · Holiday planner

The development of the tourist industry can bring many benefits. For tourists it can improve the chances of having a good holiday. For the areas and countries involved it can be an important source of money and employment. Places like Spain, Greece and Italy that were once very poor now have much higher standards of living due to increased tourism. Countries in the poorer developing world have followed their lead. Kenya, Egypt, India and the islands of the Caribbean, for example, have used money from tourism to improve their quality of life by building new schools, hospitals, roads and factories. Some of the money has also been spent on further developing the tourist industry.

Some of the benefits that the tourist industry may bring are shown on the suitcase labels below.

C

- NEW PLACES TO VISIT
- DEMAND FOR LOCALLY PRODUCED FOOD
- OLD BUILDINGS GET REPAIRED
- JOBS IN HOTELS, RESTAURANTS, ETC
- MONEY FOR HOSPITALS, SCHOOLS, ETC.
- DEMAND FOR LOCALLY PRODUCED SOUVENIRS
- BRINGS NEW IDEAS TO AREA
- NEW AMENITIES WHICH LOCALS CAN USE
- BETTER HOLIDAYS
- BRINGS IN MONEY
- IMPROVEMENTS IN TRANSPORT

Activities

1 Sort the following into **primary**, **secondary** and **tertiary**. There are two descriptions for each.
   - Provides a service
   - Something is made
   - Provides raw materials
   - Usually done in a factory
   - Product comes from the land or sea
   - Is helpful to people

2 Write down four facts about the tourist industry.

3 Which of the jobs in sketch **B** would you most like to do? Give reasons.

4 Make a list of all the different jobs that might be found in a large tourist hotel. Try to put down more than fifteen.

5 List the jobs of people in the tourist industry who have helped you at some time. Say where and when each one happened.

6 Tourist developments can help both tourists and local people. Make a copy of table **D** and sort the statements from drawing **C** into the correct columns. Some statements will appear in both columns.

D

Tourists	Local people

Summary

Tertiary industries provide a service for people. People who work in the tourist industry are part of the tertiary sector. Tourism is one of the fastest growing industries in the world today. It can bring wealth, help create jobs and provide improved facilities for local people.

What problems does tourism cause?

Over the last thirty years or so there has been a rapid increase in tourism. More people are taking holidays, many are having several holidays a year, and travel abroad is becoming increasingly popular. There are three main reasons for this. The first is that most people are now better off than in the past and have more money available for luxuries such as holidays. Secondly, people have more leisure time and the length of their annual holidays has increased. Thirdly, places have become more accessible as transport improvements have made travel faster, easier and cheaper.

This increase in tourism has brought many benefits but it has also caused problems. Photos **A** and **B** show two of these problems – attractive places spoilt by rubbish left by tourists in one case, and overcrowding in the other. Many places that hoped to gain from tourism have been disappointed. Some of the reasons for this disappointment are given below.

- The better tourist jobs rarely go to local people.
- Jobs are seasonal so there is no work for much of the year.
- Tourism raises prices so locals cannot afford goods in shops.
- Locals cannot afford to use tourist facilities.
- Discos, bars and other tourist attractions spoil the local way of life.
- Most of the money from tourism goes out of the area.

Some of the worst problems occur in the countryside. People go there for peace and quiet, and to enjoy the views. Unfortunately, they can spoil the very environment that they were attracted to in the first place. Below are some of the problems caused by tourism in the countryside. See if you can spot them and any others on cartoon **C**.

- Narrow country roads are blocked by traffic.
- Attractive landscapes are spoilt by tourist buildings.
- Litter looks unsightly and is a danger to animals.
- Walls are knocked down by careless tourists.
- Gates are left open allowing animals to get out.
- Popular locations are overcrowded and spoilt.
- Farming land is damaged.
- Farmers are unable to go about their business.
- Wildlife is frightened away.
- Trees and plants are damaged.

Tourism will not go away. People will always want to have holidays. Holiday areas will always want to have tourists around. What we need to do is to plan and manage the tourist industry carefully. We must try to increase the good effects but reduce the bad ones.

A A tourist area spoilt by litter

B An overcrowded tourist resort

Activities

1 Give three reasons for the increase in tourism.

2 The results of tourism can be disappointing for some places. Six reasons for this are given on page 40. Copy table **D** and put each reason in the correct column.

Money	Jobs	Others

D

3 **a)** Match each of the labels from drawing **E** with the correct number from cartoon **C**.
 b) Which four do you think would cause most problems for farmers in the area? Give reasons for each of your answers.
 c) Which four do you think would most spoil the area for tourists? Give reasons for each of your answers.

E

LITTER

DAMAGED WALLS — DIFFICULTIES FOR FARMERS

OVERCROWDING — GATES LEFT OPEN

DAMAGE TO VEGETATION — SPOILT LANDSCAPE

DAMAGED FARMLAND — LOSS OF WILDLIFE

EXTRA

Choose any two of the problems shown in cartoon **C**. For each one suggest what might be done to prevent it or at least reduce its bad effects.

Summary

Tourist activities can bring enjoyment and create employment and wealth. In some places tourism can cause problems for people and spoil the environment. Care is needed in planning and managing tourist environments.

What are National Parks?

National Parks are large areas of beautiful countryside. Their scenery and wildlife are protected so that everyone can enjoy them. The world's first Park was opened as long ago as 1872 at Yellowstone in the United States. Since then many countries have set up similar Parks. Parks around the world vary in many ways but they all have the same two aims.

1 To preserve and care for the environment.

2 To provide a place for recreation and enjoyment.

Britain's first National Parks were set up in the 1950s. At that time the government felt there was a real danger that some of Britain's finest scenery would be damaged or permanently destroyed. The main idea of the Parks was to provide protection for the environment. It was also hoped that they would help to look after the way of life and livelihood of people already living there. These included people working on farms, in forestry and in various other activities.

The National Park Authorities have a difficult task. The Parks cover a very large area. Nearly a quarter of a million people live in them and they have over 90 million visits each year. Each Park employs staff who are experts in planning, conservation and land management. **Park rangers** do an important job. They help visitors to get the most out of the Parks and ensure that the landscape is protected. Volunteers are encouraged to help look after the Parks. These often include students from schools and colleges who work at weekends or during their holidays.

Sketch **A** shows some ways in which the Parks protect the countryside and help local people and visitors.

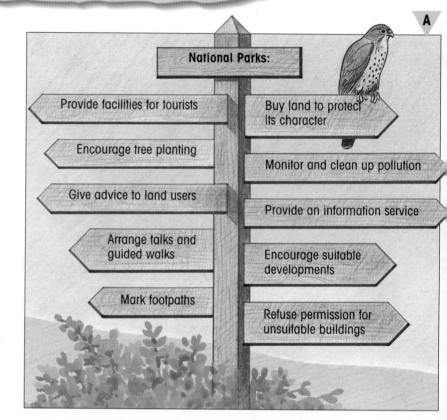

A

National Parks:

Provide facilities for tourists

Encourage tree planting

Give advice to land users

Arrange talks and guided walks

Mark footpaths

Buy land to protect its character

Monitor and clean up pollution

Provide an information service

Encourage suitable developments

Refuse permission for unsuitable buildings

B Orrest Head, Windermere

1. Preserve and care for the environment

2. To provide a place for recreation and enjoyment

42

C National Parks in England and Wales

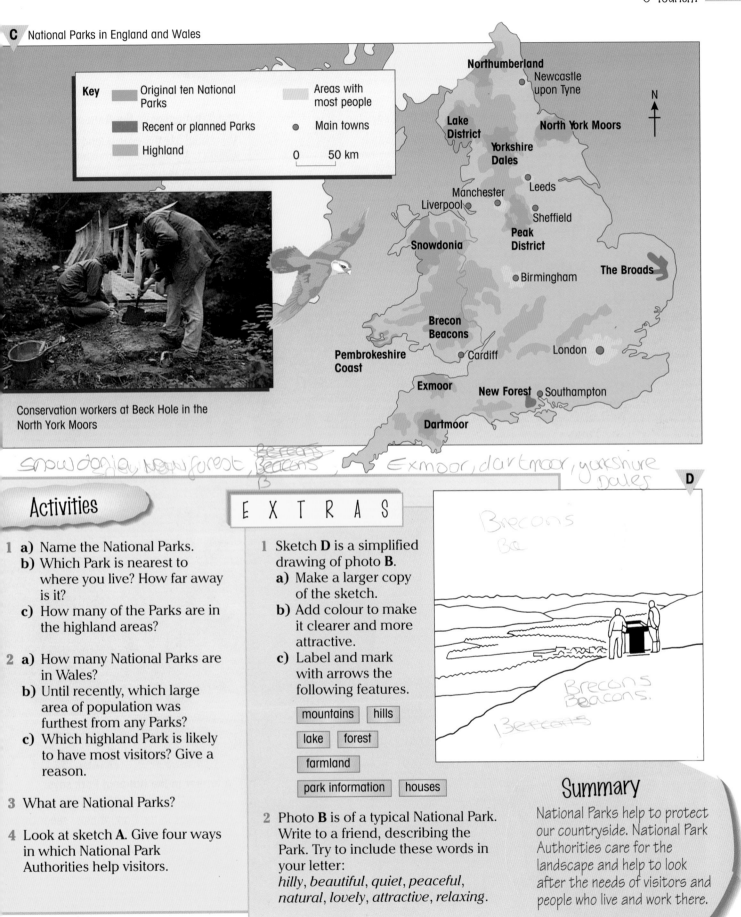

Key
- Original ten National Parks
- Recent or planned Parks
- Highland
- Areas with most people
- Main towns

0   50 km

Northumberland
Newcastle upon Tyne
Lake District
North York Moors
Yorkshire Dales
Leeds
Manchester
Liverpool
Sheffield
Snowdonia
Peak District
Birmingham
The Broads
Brecon Beacons
Cardiff
London
Pembrokeshire Coast
Exmoor
New Forest   Southampton
Dartmoor

N

Conservation workers at Beck Hole in the North York Moors

snowdonia, new forest, Brecon Beacons, Exmoor, dartmoor, yorkshire Dales (handwritten)

Activities

1 **a)** Name the National Parks.
b) Which Park is nearest to where you live? How far away is it?
c) How many of the Parks are in the highland areas?

2 **a)** How many National Parks are in Wales?
b) Until recently, which large area of population was furthest from any Parks?
c) Which highland Park is likely to have most visitors? Give a reason.

3 What are National Parks?

4 Look at sketch **A**. Give four ways in which National Park Authorities help visitors.

snowdonia (handwritten)

E X T R A S

1 Sketch **D** is a simplified drawing of photo **B**.
a) Make a larger copy of the sketch.
b) Add colour to make it clearer and more attractive.
c) Label and mark with arrows the following features.

| mountains | hills |

| lake | forest |

| farmland |

| park information | houses |

2 Photo **B** is of a typical National Park. Write to a friend, describing the Park. Try to include these words in your letter:
hilly, beautiful, quiet, peaceful, natural, lovely, attractive, relaxing.

D

Brecons Bc (handwritten)
Brecons Beacons. (handwritten)
Beacons (handwritten)

Summary

National Parks help to protect our countryside. National Park Authorities care for the landscape and help to look after the needs of visitors and people who live and work there.

What is conflict?

Ramblers in the National Park say:

'The National Park provides us with a wonderful sense of freedom away from the restrictions of everyday life. We feel we should be able to camp, picnic or walk wherever we like. After all it is a National Park, isn't it?'

Conservationists in the National Park say:

'We would like the superb landscape and wildlife to be looked after properly. We worry that flowers don't grow because they are nibbled by too many sheep, and birds don't nest because of too many people and dogs. W must make sure that we care for our Parks. In this way they will continue to be special places for both local people and visitors.'

A ranger in the National Park says:

'I advise visitors to the Park about where they can or cannot go. I encourage them to respect and understand nature and the needs of the people who live and work here. I also talk with Park residents, especially those who have problems caused by visitors. Another part of my job is actually looking after the Park. This includes mending fences, marking foot-paths and looking after wildlife sites.'

A farmer in the National Park says:

'I can understand that people like to enjoy themselves in the Park. It must seem very beautiful and peaceful to people used to the big cities. Visitors should realise, however, that this is my home and I have to make a living here. Uncontrolled dogs running amongst my sheep, or field gates left open, are a constant worry. I can't afford to lose my sheep or have my land damaged.'

The page opposite shows some of the problems people have in National Parks. These problems can cause **conflict**. Conflict is when there is disagreement over how something should be used.

Land ownership is a main cause of conflict in the Parks. As graph **A** shows, very little of the land is owned by the nation for everyone to use and enjoy. Most of it belongs to private individuals like farmers and house owners. Farmers may not want tourists to walk across their land. House owners may not like visitors parking outside their houses and blocking drives or leaving litter.

An important job of the National Park rangers is to try to reduce this conflict for the benefit of all concerned.

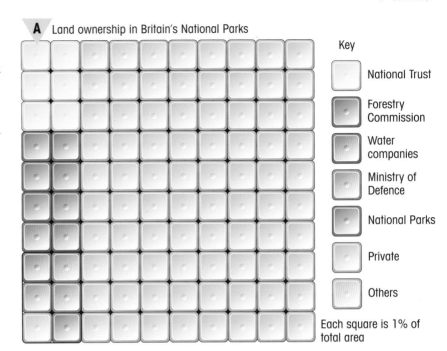

A Land ownership in Britain's National Parks

Key

National Trust

Forestry Commission

Water companies

Ministry of Defence

National Parks

Private

Others

Each square is 1% of total area

Activities

1 What is conflict?

2 Conflict arises in National Parks between people in many ways. The pictures in **B** show some of these people. Match up the pictures with the statements numbered **1** to **6**.

3 Look at graph **A**.
 a) What percentage of land is privately owned?
 b) How much land is owned by National Parks?
 c) Who are the second largest land owners?
 d) Which land owner may cause most conflict with tourists? Give reasons.

E X T R A

You will need to work with someone else for this activity. Discuss whether the following should be allowed in National Parks. Write down reasons for your answers.
1 Motor cycle scrambling
2 Motor boat racing
3 Mountain bikes
4 A motorway
5 A leisure park

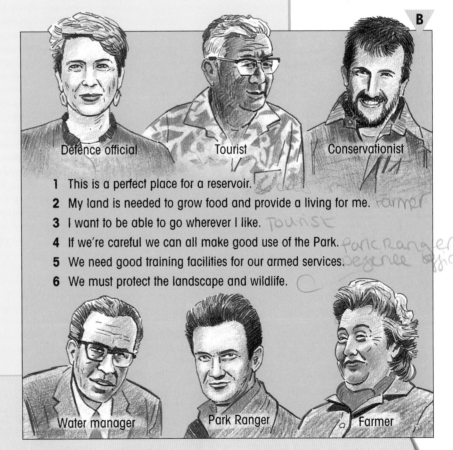

B

Defence official   Tourist   Conservationist

1 This is a perfect place for a reservoir. ~~Water manager~~
2 My land is needed to grow food and provide a living for me. Farmer
3 I want to be able to go wherever I like. Tourist
4 If we're careful we can all make good use of the Park. Park Ranger
5 We need good training facilities for our armed services. Defence official
6 We must protect the landscape and wildlife. Conservationist

Water manager   Park Ranger   Farmer

Summary The needs of different people can cause conflict in areas of attractive countryside. Careful management by National Park Authorities can help reduce the problem.

Tourism in Europe

Western Europe is one of the world's most developed tourist areas. Countries here are relatively small and close together. Travel is fast and efficient and the high standards of living mean that people have more money to spend on their holidays. Most tourist movement in Europe is from the cool north to the sunshine and warmth of the south. By far the most popular areas are the countries of the Mediterranean where hot sun and blue skies are common through the months of July and August. The mountainous areas of Europe, especially those with heavy snowfall like the Alps, have become increasingly popular for skiing and other winter sports.

Map **A** shows some of Europe's most popular tourist places. The reasons for their popularity are given in the boxes below the map.

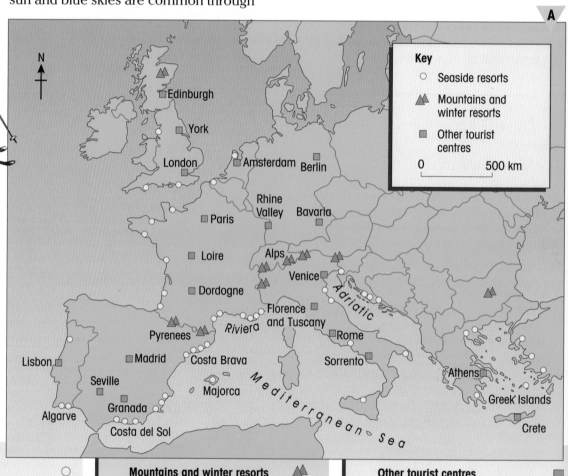

A

Key
- ○ Seaside resorts
- ▲▲ Mountains and winter resorts
- ■ Other tourist centres

0 ——— 500 km

Seaside holiday resorts ○

These are mainly along the Mediterranean coastline. Some reasons for their popularity are:

- ○ Hot, dry and sunny summers
- ○ Beaches for sun-bathing and children's play
- ○ Warm sea for swimming and water sports
- ○ Interesting cliff scenery for coastal walks
- ○ Hotels, nightlife and other holiday activities.

Mountains and winter resorts ▲▲

The Alps are the most popular mountain area for tourists. The Pyrenees also attracts many visitors. People go to these places mainly for:

- ▲ Spectacular scenery
- ▲ Walking and climbing holidays
- ▲ Skiing and winter sports
- ▲ Peace, quiet and fresh air.

Other tourist centres ■

People like to visit places that are interesting and different to what they are used to. Some of the things that attract tourists are:

- ■ Interesting towns and villages
- ■ Old buildings, castles, cathedrals and museums
- ■ Historic sites
- ■ Leisure parks
- ■ A different way of life.

Map **B** shows the ten most popular European destinations for British tourists. The thickness of each line shows the number of tourists going to that country. A map like this is called a **flow map**. Notice which are the most popular areas. Why do you think the north of Europe has so few visitors?

Tourism has affect Europe in many ways. New motorways, rail links and airports have been built to improve travel. New resorts have been constructed and old, interesting buildings improved to attract tourists. Table **C** shows that tourism has also provided employment and brought in large amounts of money to many countries.

As we have seen, however, tourism is not all good news. Some places have been badly affected by unsuitable developments. These have spoilt the surroundings and caused problems for people.

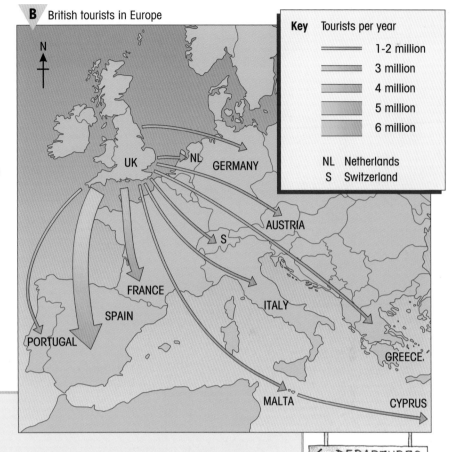

B British tourists in Europe

Key	Tourists per year
	1-2 million
	3 million
	4 million
	5 million
	6 million

NL Netherlands
S Switzerland

Activities

1 List the following in the order that you think is the most important for a good holiday.

historic places • beaches • scenery • good weather • new places • different language • walks • things to do

2 Look at map **A**.
   a) Use the scale line to measure the distances from London to each of the places below.

   Paris • Majorca • Rome • The Alps • Athens • The Pyrenees • Greek Islands

   b) Sort the places under the headings **Seaside**, **Mountains**, **Others**. Add three more places to each heading.

3 Look at flow map **B**.
   a) How many British tourists went to Spain for their holidays? Was it 1.2 million, 4.0 million or 6.2 million?
   b) Which two countries were most popular with British tourists?
   c) Suggest three reasons for their popularity.

4 Given a free choice, which place in Europe would you most like to visit? Give reasons for your answer.

EXTRA

Draw a bar graph to show the money earned by countries from tourism.
- Arrange the bars in order of size with the biggest on the left.
- Colour the countries with a Mediterranean coastline in yellow and the rest in green.
- Give your graph a key and title.
- Describe what the graph shows.

C

Income from tourism	£ billion
France	7.3
Germany	4.8
Greece	1.4
Italy	7.5
Netherlands	1.7
Portugal	1.4
Spain	9.1
UK	6.3

Summary

Tourism is one of Europe's most important industries. The most popular areas are in the south where the main attraction is good weather. Mountain areas are becoming increasingly popular as all-year-round holiday destinations.

Majorca — a holiday paradise?

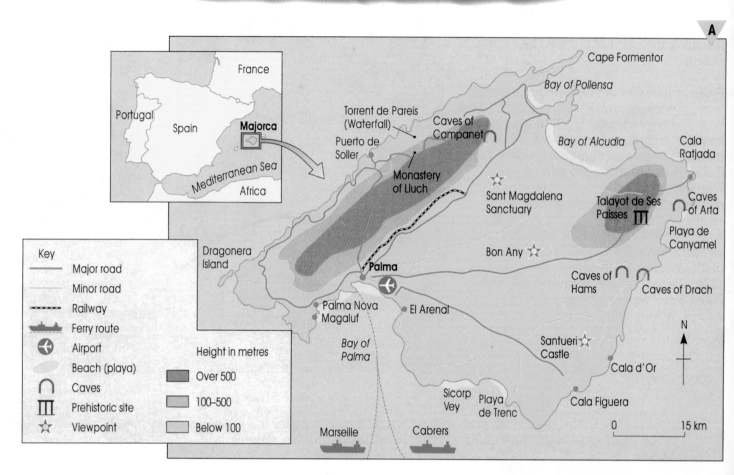

A

Key
- Major road
- Minor road
- Railway
- Ferry route
- Airport
- Beach (playa)
- Caves
- Prehistoric site
- Viewpoint

Height in metres
- Over 500
- 100–500
- Below 100

The Spanish island of Majorca is the largest of the Balearic Islands and lies about 200 kilometres off the east coast of Spain. Many people consider it to be the most beautiful of all the Mediterranean islands. On the right is part of a travel brochure which describes the island.

In 1991 over 5 million tourists visited Majorca. The island has a permanent population of 520,000 and measures little more than 80 square kilometres. It is not surprising that the effects of tourism can be seen everywhere.

Some of the effects are bad. Many islanders worry about the noise, litter, violence and drunkenness that has become common in some of the more developed areas. They also worry about the effects of tourism on Spanish culture and traditions. They argue that many of the jobs provided are unskilled, poorly paid and seasonal.

Most islanders, however, are willing to put up with the problems caused by tourism. They are grateful for any employment opportunities that come their way. They feel that the money that tourism brings to the island more than balances the damage that comes with it.

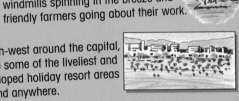

Majorca

In the north, rugged mountains covered with pine, cork, almond and olive trees overlook the deep blue sea.

In the east is a spectacular coastline with towering cliffs and lots of golden, sandy beaches.

Inland are tiny white farms, quaint windmills spinning in the breeze and friendly farmers going about their work.

In the south-west around the capital, Palma, are some of the liveliest and most developed holiday resort areas you can find anywhere.

All round the island is the Mediterranean Sea — warm, clear and inviting. Add to this a climate that in summer brings week after week of hot weather and brilliant blue skies and you have what can only be described as a holiday paradise.

B The unspoilt North

C The developed South

Activities

1 Make a Fact File using the headings shown below. Add any other things about Majorca that interest you.

Fact file

Name of islands _____
Distance from Spain _____
Population _____
Capital _____
Weather _____
Size _____
Physical features _____
Vegetation _____
Tourists per year _____

2 Look at photos **B** and **C**. Sort the following under the headings **Unspoilt North** and **Developed South**. Some may go under both headings.

Hot, sunny weather, many tourists, crowded, open spaces, noisy, many hotels, nightlife, lovely views, beaches, peace and quiet, farmland.

3 **a)** Write down the good effects of tourism for Majorca.
b) List at least six problems that tourism has caused in Majorca.

4 Look carefully at map **A**.
a) Make a list of all the things that interest you and the places you would like to visit.
b) Plan how you would spend a week in Majorca. Describe what you would do and see on each day.

E X T R A

Produce a small booklet about Majorca. Try to include:
■ a map and description of where it is
■ a simple map of the island
■ a page on its natural attractions
■ a page on tourist developments
■ a page to show the advantages and disadvantages that tourism has brought.

You may be able to get some ideas and photos from a travel brochure.

Summary

Majorca is the Mediterranean's most popular holiday island. Its attractions include spectacular scenery, glorious weather and lively seaside resorts. Some people are concerned about the bad effects of tourism.

49

Disneyland Paris — a holiday dream?

A

Disney leisure resorts are known throughout the world. They were first developed in the 1950s by Walt Disney. His idea was to provide fun, thrills and adventure for people by building a world of dreams, fantasies and make-believe.

The first Disneyland opened in California in 1955. This was followed by Florida's Magic Kingdom in 1971 and Tokyo Disneyland in 1983. In the early 1980s it was decided to build a resort in Europe which would be called Euro Disney. Much time was spent choosing the best possible location. Places in Britain, Germany, Italy, Spain and France were considered. There were four main requirements that the site had to meet.

1 There needed to be a large local **population**.
2 The area already had to be popular with **tourists**.
3 **Transport** systems and accessibility had to be good.
4 A large area of **land** had to be available.

Eventually in 1985 a site near Paris was chosen for reasons shown on map **B** below. Building started in 1988 and the grand opening was held in April 1992. About 11 million people a year visit Disneyland ® Paris, as it is now known. This makes it Europe's greatest tourist attraction.

Disneyland Paris has been good for the people of Paris. Already it has increased tourism and brought money to the city. It has also brought about transport improvements and in its first year alone it created 12,000 new jobs. As well as these benefits, Disneyland Paris also provides fun and enjoyment for the many Parisians who visit the resort in their own leisure time.

B

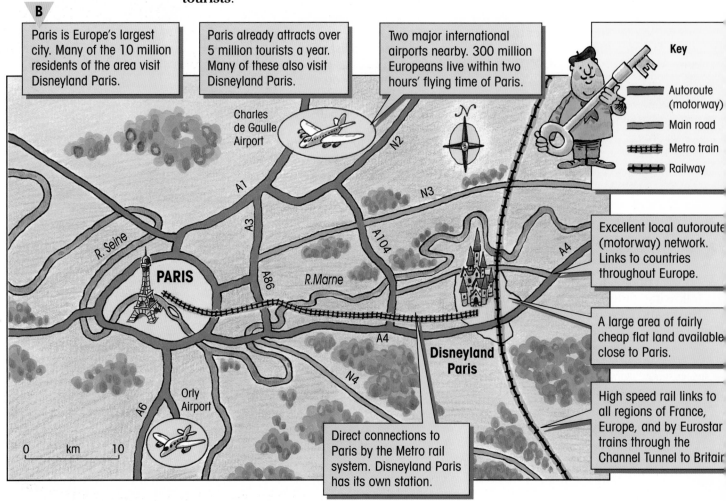

Paris is Europe's largest city. Many of the 10 million residents of the area visit Disneyland Paris.

Paris already attracts over 5 million tourists a year. Many of these also visit Disneyland Paris.

Two major international airports nearby. 300 million Europeans live within two hours' flying time of Paris.

Key
— Autoroute (motorway)
— Main road
++++ Metro train
++++ Railway

Charles de Gaulle Airport

N2

N3

A1

A3

R. Seine

PARIS

A86

A104

R. Marne

A4

Excellent local autoroute (motorway) network. Links to countries throughout Europe.

A large area of fairly cheap flat land available close to Paris.

Disneyland Paris

N4

Orly Airport

A6

0   km   10

Direct connections to Paris by the Metro rail system. Disneyland Paris has its own station.

High speed rail links to all regions of France, Europe, and by Eurostar trains through the Channel Tunnel to Britain

C

Disneyland® Paris is a theme park. It is made up of five different 'lands', each following a theme or idea. Each land has its own attractions. These include rides, shows, shops, restaurants and hotels. All the time there is live entertainment going on and activities to take part in.

Outside the 'theme lands' there are many other attractions. These include a golf course, tennis courts, an evening entertainment centre, and an ice-skating rink. Hotels, a camp site and several self-catering retreats provide accommodation.

Main Street USA shows what a street in America looked like a hundred years ago. There are interesting shops, antique cars and horse-drawn carriages. Musicians entertain on the sidewalks.

Frontierland shows life in the American West. There are cowboy 'shoot-outs' a haunted mansion, steamboat trips and a thrilling rail journey through mountains and down a mine shaft.

Adventureland features an attack by pirates on a Caribbean port. Here are also smugglers, an 'Adventure Island' and all the excitement of an oriental bazaar.

Fantasyland is the world of fairy tales and make believe. The Sleeping Beauty Castle is the centrepiece. Snow White, Mickey Mouse and other characters provide the entertainment.

Discoveryland is the world of the future. Its spectacular special effects include a trip across the universe, a Star Wars adventure and a Michael Jackson 3D musical.

© Disney

Activities

1 a) Where and when did the first Disneyland open?
   b) Name three other places with Disney resorts.
   c) What was Walt Disney's idea?

2 a) Name two Paris airports.
   b) Which autoroute links Paris with Disneyland Paris?
   c) How far is it by Metro train from Paris to Disneyland Paris?

3 Describe three different ways by which you could travel from Britain to Disneyland Paris.

4 Make a large copy of diagram **D**. Add examples from the Paris area for each location factor. One has been done for you.

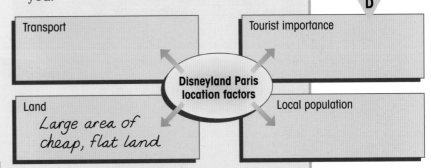

D

Transport

Tourist importance

Disneyland Paris location factors

Land
Large area of cheap, flat land

Local population

E X T R A

Plan a trip to Disneyland Paris for a group of friends. Describe how you will get there, where you will stay and what you will do. Write a postcard home.

Summary Disneyland Paris has been located near Paris because of good transport, a large population, existing tourism and suitable land.

The Alps — a winter wonderland?

A

"We live in La Clusaz in the French Alps. Our village is very pretty. It is nestled in a valley and surrounded by high mountains. The area is very popular with tourists. They come to view the spectacular scenery and enjoy the fresh air. People also like the traditional way of life here which is unspoilt and very French.

The area is popular throughout the year but the busiest time is February and March when the skiers come. In those months La Clusaz is packed with tourists and is full of activity. We have 56 ski lifts in our valley and employ 150 ski instructors. The skiing is fantastic and we even have 16 mountain restaurants for people who want to stay on the slopes all day.

There is probably more to do in the village in winter than in summer. There are plenty of bars, nightclubs and restaurants for adults. We like to visit the ice rink or swimming pool. Sometimes we go to one of the four discos. The best one is L'Ecluse. It is built over a floodlit stream."

"La Clusaz is much better now than it used to be. When our parents were young all the people around here were farmers and there was nothing at all for young people to do. Most young people had to leave the area to get jobs. Now there is plenty for us to do, lots of people to meet and we can get jobs in the tourist industry."

Key

	Alps
●	Main towns
L	Luxembourg
NL	Netherlands

0   100   200 km

N

UK
London
NL
BELGIUM
L
GERMANY
Paris
FRANCE
SWITZERLAND
Geneva
Lyon
La Clusaz
ITALY
Bordeaux
Marseille
Mediterranean Sea
SPAIN

B   La Clusaz in winter

C   Summer tennis coaching at La Clusaz

66 In our village we are very careful to look after what we have and make sure that it is not spoilt. We know from talking to friends in other villages that some places have problems.

In a valley not far from here the clearing of forest to make more ski runs caused landslides and floods. Rocks and trees hurtled down the slopes and blocked the river. Houses and roads were destroyed and farm land was ruined. The buildings and roads can be repaired but the farmers' land may be damaged for many years to come. The mountain slopes will never recover (photo **D**).

Overcrowding and congestion is also a problem. Skiing is so popular now that there just isn't room for everyone. Some resorts are putting a limit on how many skiers they can take. When that limit is reached they simply close the mountain.

We think that most of the problems can be sorted out. La Clusaz already has strict planning controls. New building can only take place with special permission, and plans for extra ski lifts are very carefully considered. **99**

D Damage due to increased flooding in the French Alps

Activities

1 **a)** In which countries are the Alps?
  b) Name the three main towns nearest to La Clusaz.
  c) How far is it from London to La Clusaz?

2 The main attractions of La Clusaz are:
  - fine scenery
  - mountains
  - entertainments
  - wildlife
  - wild flowers
  - skiing area
  - restaurants
  - outdoor activities
  - attractive village
  - shops

  List which of these you can see in photos **B** and **C**.

3 Make a list of tourist industry jobs that may be available at La Clusaz. You should write down at least eight, but try to make a really long list.

4 **a)** Make a copy of table **E**.
  b) Tick the correct boxes for each effect of tourism.
  c) Colour the benefits in green and the problems in red.
  d) Choose any one problem and suggest what could be done to reduce it.

E X T R A

Design a page for a travel brochure advertising La Clusaz as a ski resort. Include information on location, skiing and other attractions. Make your page as interesting, colourful and attractive as possible.

E

Effect	People	Environment
New jobs		
Traffic jams		
Overcrowding		
Things to do		
Loss of wildlife		
People to meet		
Soil erosion		
Flooding		
Increased wealth		

Summary

Mountain areas are becoming increasingly popular with tourists. Europe's alpine resorts attract large numbers of winter visitors. Care needs to be taken to protect the surroundings.

What is the European Union?

The European Union, or EU in short, is a group of countries trying to work together. It began when six countries joined together to try to build up their industries and improve their economies following the Second World War (**A**). Since then it has expanded in two ways (map **B**).

1 The number of member countries has increased to fifteen. More countries, especially in Eastern Europe, are likely to apply to join in the next few years.

2 Its activities have grown from trade and industry to include finance, tourism and care of the environment. Other activities are shown in diagram **C**.

A

History of the EU

1951 The European Iron and Steel Community was formed

1957 Six countries signed the Treaty of Rome creating the European Economic Community or 'Common Market'

1973 Membership increased to nine countries – including the UK

1981 Ten members

1986 The EC enlarged to twelve countries

1993 The single market

1995 The EU enlarged to fifteen countries

B Members of the EU at the beginning of 1997

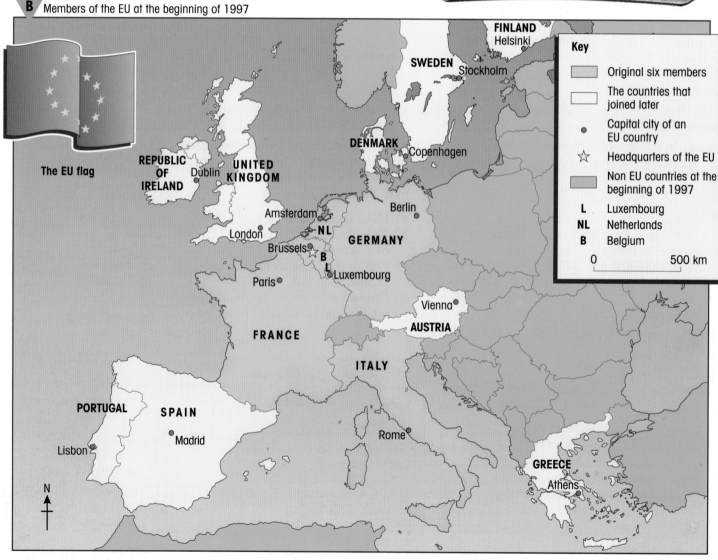

The EU flag

Key

Original six members

The countries that joined later

• Capital city of an EU country

☆ Headquarters of the EU

Non EU countries at the beginning of 1997

L Luxembourg
NL Netherlands
B Belgium

0   500 km

C What does the EU do?

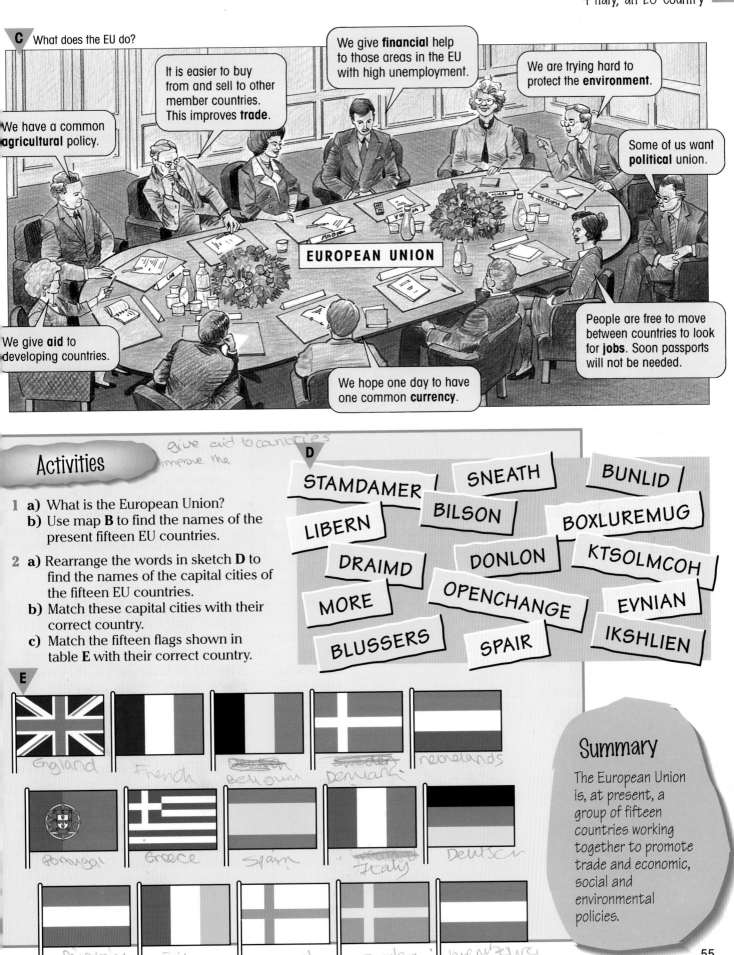

We have a common **agricultural** policy.

It is easier to buy from and sell to other member countries. This improves **trade**.

We give **financial** help to those areas in the EU with high unemployment.

We are trying hard to protect the **environment**.

Some of us want **political** union.

EUROPEAN UNION

We give **aid** to developing countries.

We hope one day to have one common **currency**.

People are free to move between countries to look for **jobs**. Soon passports will not be needed.

Activities

give aid to countries
improve the

1 a) What is the European Union?
   b) Use map **B** to find the names of the present fifteen EU countries.

2 a) Rearrange the words in sketch **D** to find the names of the capital cities of the fifteen EU countries.
   b) Match these capital cities with their correct country.
   c) Match the fifteen flags shown in table **E** with their correct country.

D

STAMDAMER | SNEATH | BUNLID
LIBERN | BILSON | BOXLUREMUG
DRAIMD | DONLON | KTSOLMCOH
MORE | OPENCHANGE | EVNIAN
BLUSSERS | SPAIR | IKSHLIEN

E

England | French | Belgium | Denmark | netherlands

Portugal | Greece | Spain | Italy | Deutsch

Austria | Ireland | Finland | Sweden | Luxembourg

Summary

The European Union is, at present, a group of fifteen countries working together to promote trade and economic, social and environmental policies.

55

What gives Italy its sense of identity?

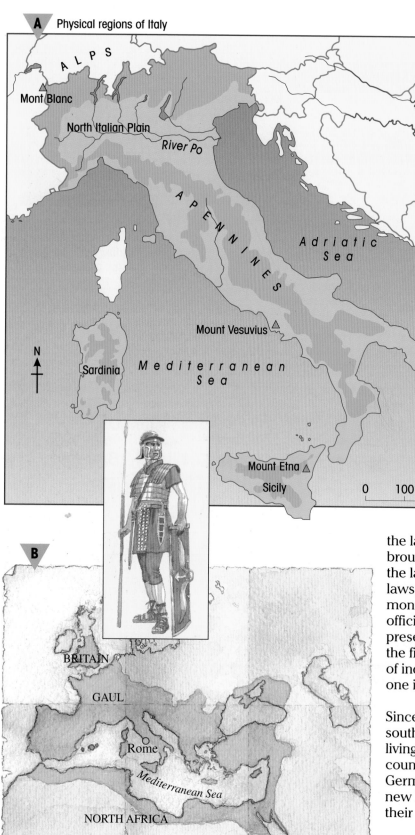

A Physical regions of Italy

ALPS
Mont Blanc
North Italian Plain
River Po
APENNINES
Adriatic Sea
Mont Blanc
Mediterranean Sea
Sardinia
Mount Vesuvius
N
Mount Etna
Sicily

0   100   200 km

Italy is a **peninsula** which stretches out into the Mediterranean Sea. A peninsula is a piece of land surrounded on three sides by the sea. Italy can be divided into three different regions.

1 In the extreme north of the country are Europe's highest mountains, the Alps (map **A**). Mont Blanc, Europe's highest mountain, is on the border between Italy and France.
2 Most of the peninsula, and the two Italian islands of Sicily and Sardinia, are mountainous. This part of Italy has a **Mediterranean** climate and includes two famous **volcanoes** – Etna and Vesuvius (pages 20–23). Many parts of the Apennines, which form a mountainous backbone to the peninsula, are bare due to deforestation and **soil erosion** (pages 32–33).
3 The only large area of lowland is the **North Italian Plain**. It lies to the south of the Alps and is drained by the River Po and its tributaries.

Italy and the Italians

Two thousand years ago the country which is now called Italy was part of the large Roman Empire (map **B**). The Romans brought civilisation to much of Western Europe and the lands around the Mediterranean Sea. They made laws, enforced peace and built roads, cities and monuments. They spoke Latin. This became the official language of their empire and was the origin of present day Italian. The Roman Empire collapsed in the fifth century. From then until 1870 Italy was a group of individual states. In 1870 Italy re-united and became one independent country.

Since then many Italians, especially those living in the south of the country, have found it hard to earn a living. Large numbers have **migrated** to other countries. Some moved to find work in nearby Germany and Switzerland. Others moved to start a new life in America and Australia. They took with them their culture and characteristics.

B

BRITAIN
GAUL
Rome
Mediterranean Sea
NORTH AFRICA

Different groups of people tend to develop their own customs and way of life. This can include their language and religion, how they dress and behave, what they eat and what they do in their spare time. This creates a sense of identity.

The photos in **C** show some ways in which Italians have developed a sense of identity.

If we put these characteristics together for Italy we get a mental picture of typical, or **stereotype**, Italians. We must, however, remember that there are many types of Italians. They are not all the same as the people shown below.

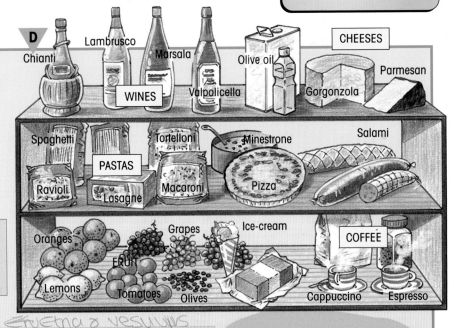

C

> We spend more money on food and drink than any other EU country.

> We have strong family links. We like children and we look after the elderly.

> Most of us are religious and are Roman Catholics.

> I like music, especially opera, and clothes.

> I like sport, especially motor racing and football.

> We are cheerful and like talking. We often get excited and emotional.

> We have produced many famous painters, sculptors, inventors, composers and writers.

Activities

Sardinia
Etna & Vesuvius

1 On a simple map of Italy mark on and name the Alps and the Apennines, three mountains, two islands and the River Po.

2 Using the photos in **C**, suggest how members of an Italian family might spend a weekend.

3 Using diagram **D** make up a menu for a typical Italian meal.

> Choice of starter, choice of main dish; choice of dessert; drink during and after the meal

D

Chianti — Lambrusco — Marsala — Olive oil — **CHEESES**
WINES — Valpolicella — Gorgonzola — Parmesan

Spaghetti — Tortelloni — Minestrone — Salami
PASTAS
Ravioli — Lasagne — Macaroni — Pizza

Oranges — Grapes — Ice-cream — **COFFEE**
FRUIT
Lemons — Tomatoes — Olives — Cappuccino — Espresso

Try to find out when these Italians lived and why they are famous: Michelangelo, St Francis of Assisi, Alberto Tomba, Dante, Julius Caesar, Mussolini, Christopher Columbus, Galileo, Hadrian, Vivaldi, Pavarotti, Marconi, Romulus, Riccardo Patrese, Augustus Caesar, Marco Polo, Leonardo da Vinci, Verdi, Sophia Loren, the Benetton brothers.

Summary

Each country has its own history and develops its own customs and way of life. These combine to give the country a sense of identity.

How does the environment affect people?

One of the earliest settled parts of Italy was around Mount Vesuvius and the Gulf of Naples (map **A**, page 56). The soil around the mountain was perfect for farming and the sea allowed people to trade. It was not until Vesuvius erupted in AD79 and destroyed the towns of Pompeii and Herculaneum (sketch **A**) that people realised it was a volcano. The ruins of these Roman towns and the Mediterranean climate now attract many tourists (page 16). Apart from tourism, most people find jobs as farmers or work in the large city of Naples.

To the south, the Sorrento peninsula is very different. The rock is limestone which gives hilly land and poor soil. Most of the area is covered in typical Mediterranean scrub vegetation (page 18). Along the south coast there is hardly any flat land. Hillsides have been terraced for farming. Several small, attractive holiday resorts cling to the cliffs and are linked by a single narrow, twisting road (photo **B**).

It is the climate and the local differences in relief and soils which are mainly responsible for the occupations, land use and settlement pattern of the area.

A

N

Old volcanoes

Suburbs

Inner city. Old tenements built close together.

Nucleated settlement. CBD noisy and congested.

Mount Vesuvius 1,281 m

Small factories in industrial zone and port

NAPLES

Port

Polluted sea

Coastal road (autostrad and railway

Herculaneum — destroyed by mud flows when Vesuvius erupted in AD79

Linear settlement along coast. 'Suburban' type houses.

B

Ship-building

GULF OF NAPLES

Sorrento — holiday resort with houses in a line along cliff-tops

Road

Hydrofoil

Coastal road – 30 with 750 major be

Capri – tourist resort

C

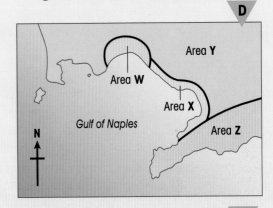

An **infrared** photo taken from a **Landsat** satellite as it circles the earth at a height of 900 km.

Landing at Naples Airport

1 Old lava flows

2 Mediterranean scrub

3 Mediterranean woodland with dispersed farms and vineyards. Sparsely populated.

Ash and lava weather into a fertile soil

Many small farms. Intensive farming of fruit, vegetables, olives and vines. Irrigation in summer. Densely populated.

Pompeii – destroyed by falling ash in AD79 eruption. Now a tourist attraction.

Limestone hills, thin soil

Fruit and vines on steep, terraced hillsides

Mediterranean scrub

Amalfi – tourist resort with houses grouped together

Clean sea

Activities

1 The area shown on sketch **A** can be divided into four parts. These have been labelled **W**, **X**, **Y** and **Z** on map **D**.
   a) Make a larger copy of table **E** and complete it by using the information given on these two pages.

D

Area Y

Area W

Area X

Gulf of Naples

Area Z

N

E

	Area W	Area X	Area Y	Area Z
Settlement (e.g. dispersed, linear, nucleated)				
Land use (e.g. built-up, farming, scrub)				
Jobs (e.g. tourism, farming, factories)				

b) Give two reasons why farming is better in Area **Y** than Area **Z**.
c) Suggest why the settlement patterns in Areas **X** and **Z** are different.

2 A Landsat photo shows false colours. Using photo **C** and sketch **A**, match the following Landsat colours with the correct type of land use.

Black	Volcanic lava
Blue	Built-up areas
Reddish-brown	Rough grazing and scrub
Bright red	Sea and lakes
Pale green/brown	Crops

Summary

The main occupations, land use and settlement patterns of a locality can often be explained by its environment.

What are Italy's main regions?

What is a region? The term **region** has been used several times without explaining what it means. A region is an area of land which has common characteristics. It is therefore different to other regions. These characteristics can be:

- **Physical**, where places have the same climate, vegetation or soils.
- **Human** and **economic**, such as political areas or places with the same economic activities or level of development.

① **Mountains and lakes.** The snow-covered Alps are ideal for skiing in winter and climbing in summer. The peaceful lakes are surrounded by scented pinewoods, high mountains and attractive villages.

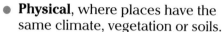

A Tourist regions of Italy

① Mountains and lakes
Venice
② North Italy and Venice
The No...
③ Italian Riviera
③ Adriatic Riviera
Florence
④ Tuscany and Rome
Rome

③ **Italian and Adriatic Rivieras.** In the west the Alps reach the sea giving headlands, cliffs and sandy bays. The Adriatic coast is noted for its wide golden beaches, watersports, lively nightlife and excellent food.

④ **Tuscany and Rome.** Famous for its art, history and scenery. Tuscany remains rural with wooded hills and large vineyards. Rome and Florence have numerous art galleries, historic buildings, fine shops and excellent food.

⑤ **Neapolitan Riviera.** Blue skies, warm and clear sea, attractive scenery, villages clinging to cliffs, and historic ruins (pages 58-9).

⑥ **The South.** Inland there are mountains and quiet, unspoilt villages. The coastal, white, sandy beaches are quiet. A place to relax (pages 62-7).

What are Italy's regions? Different people using different characteristics can produce different maps showing the regions of Italy. There is no single correct·map. For example:

- There are three main **physical** regions (map **A** page 56). These are the Alps, the North Italian Plain and the Apennines (peninsular Italy).

- There are twenty states. These **political** regions are similar to counties in Britain.
- There are two **economic** regions – the more developed North and the less developed South. The remainder of this unit describes how these two economic regions are different.
- There are seven tourist regions which are shown on these two pages.

② **North Italy and Venice.** A lowland area which has many small historic towns with their old squares and churches. In the east is Venice with its numerous canals and, nearby, long sandy beaches.

The South

⑤ ⑥ **The South**

Neapolitan Riviera

⑦ **Sicily.** The largest island in the Mediterranean. Days are usually sunny. There are remains of Greek temples, Roman theatres and Norman castles. The highlight of the attractive scenery is Mount Etna (pages 22-3).

Sicily

Activities

1 a) What is a region?
 b) What is the difference between a physical and a political region?
 c) Name three physical regions in Italy.
 d) Name the two economic regions in Italy.

2 Which region, or regions, would you visit in Italy if you wanted to:
 a) Visit art museums
 b) Ski
 c) Travel by boat on canals
 d) See a volcano
 e) Lie in the sun on a sandy beach
 f) Climb mountains
 g) Enjoy nightlife
 h) Take part in watersports
 i) See quiet villages
 j) Visit historic buildings
 k) Visit a vineyard?

3 Which of the seven tourist regions shown on map **A** would you most like to visit? Give reasons for your answer.

Summary

A region is an area of land which has common characteristics. These characteristics, which can be physical or human and economic, make each region different to other regions.

What are the physical differences between North and South Italy?

Landforms

The **North Italian Plain** was once part of the Adriatic Sea and lies between the Alps and the Apennines. Fast-flowing rivers from those highland areas brought down silt which they deposited in the shallow sea. The silt built up above sea-level forming a very flat and fertile **plain**. When snow in the Alps melts in spring the rivers may flood this low-lying land. The main river, the Po, is continually pushing its **delta** outwards into the Adriatic. Embankments have been built to try to stop it overflowing onto its flood plain (photo **A**). Little natural vegetation remains on the plain. Lombardy poplar trees have been planted to try to reduce the force of the wind.

The **South** was once part of the Mediterranean Sea. Rocks were formed on the sea bed and later pushed up to form the Apennines. These earth movements still occur today. Sometimes they cause serious **earthquakes** while at others they produce volcanic eruptions.

The steep-sided Apennines were once covered in Mediterranean woodland. When this woodland was cleared the soil was exposed to the heavy winter rain and washed away. Many parts are now either eroded (photo **B**) or covered in scrub vegetation (page 18). There is not much fertile land. The best soils are:

1 Where rivers have deposited silt as deltas at their mouths. (Most rivers are seasonal and only flow in winter.)

2 Near to volcanoes where the lava and ash soon weather into a deep soil.

A The North Italian Plain

Soil erosion in the Apennines **B**

Activities

1 Landsketches **C** and **D** show parts of the North Italian Plain and the Apennines. On large copies of these sketches put the following labels in the correct places.

Add these titles: **North Italian Plain, Apennines**.

| poplar trees | scrub vegetation | fertile silt |

| thin soil | flat plain | steep hillsides |

| permanent river | seasonal river |

| possible flooding | possible earthquake |

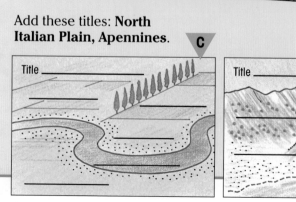

C Title _____

D Title _____

Climate

Although there are some similarities between the North Italian Plain and the South of Italy there are also many differences. These are given in table **E**.

E

	North Italian Plain	**The South**
Type of climate	Between a British and a Mediterranean climate.	Mediterranean climate (page 16)
Winter temperatures	Cold. January is between 0° and 2°C.	Warm. January is between 8° and 10°C.
Summer temperatures	Very warm. 24°C in July.	Hot. Over 26°C in July.
Rainfall	800 mm spread evenly throughout the year. Rain is usually not very heavy.	700 mm which nearly all falls in winter. Rain is usually heavy. Very little rain in summer.
Hazards	Frost is common in winter. Fog is very common at any time of year but mainly in winter (photo **F**). Milan averages 100 days of fog a year.	Drought and heatwave conditions in summer (photo **G**). Snow on higher slopes in winter.

F Venice in winter

G Sicily in the summer

H

Winters get (colder/warmer)
Summers are (hot/very hot)
Rainfall (decreases/increases)
Rain falls (all year/winter only)
(Enough/not enough) rain
(Drought/fog) is a hazard

Winters get (colder/warmer)
Summers are (hot/very hot)
Rainfall (decreases/increases)
Rain falls (all year/winter only)
(Enough/not enough) rain
(Drought/fog) is a hazard

Activities

2 Make a copy of map **H**. Add the labels by choosing the correct word from the pair in brackets to show the changes as you move north or south.

3 Give three differences between the climate of the North Italian Plain and the South of Italy in:
- summer
- winter.

Summary

There are more differences than similarities between the landscapes and climate of the North Italian Plain and the South of Italy.

Life on the North Italian Plain

The North Italian Plain is the richest region in Italy. It has a standard of living as high as anywhere in the EU. Most people live in large industrial towns and cities. Industry has attracted large numbers of workers since 1950. Some of these workers came from rural areas of the North Italian Plain (rural–urban migration) but most arrived either from the South of Italy or from poorer countries which surround the Mediterranean Sea.

Land use and jobs

Although only 4 in every 100 workers are farmers, agriculture is still a major type of land use (graph **A**). Most farms are large and the fields are grouped together, making them easier for the farmer to reach. Farming is **intensive**, meaning that no land is wasted, and **commercial**, which means that farm produce is sold for a profit. Vines are grown in the west of the region; fruit, wheat and rice in the centre; and maize (corn) in the east.

A Jobs on the North Italian Plain

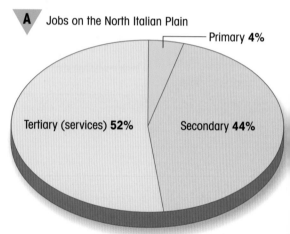

- Primary **4%**
- Secondary **44%**
- Tertiary (services) **52%**

B Advantages of the North Italian Plain for farming

| Rain falls throughout the year |
| Low-lying, flat land |
| Modern machinery |
| Plenty of money to buy fertiliser |

| Near large urban markets in northern Italy and north-west Europe |
| River Po flows all year giving water for irrigation |

| Easy to borrow money from big banks |
| Fertile silt (soil) left by River Po |
| Most farmers own their land |
| Local colleges teach modern farming methods |

Industry

The west and centre of the North Italian Plain has always been the most important industrial region in Italy. Although at first centred on the 'industrial triangle' between the cities of Turin, Milan and Genoa, it is now spreading outwards into the surrounding regions (map **D**).

The most important firm is Fiat whose large car assembly plant is in Turin (photo **C**). The present head of Fiat also owns Turin's daily newspaper and Juventus Football Club. Milan is Italy's largest city and the centre for banking and fashion. Much of the region's trade either has to pass through the port of Genoa or has to cross the Alps.

Although this is the richest part of Italy with most of the better paid and skilled jobs, it still has its problems. As more and more land is being built upon there is less for farming and recreation. Towns have grown so quickly that there has not been enough time to plan them carefully. Houses and flats have been built very close together, roads are congested and there is very little open space and parkland. There has been little care of the environment and many pollution problems have developed.

C Fiat factory, Turin

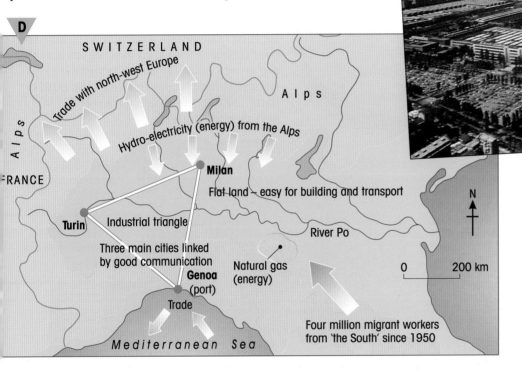

D

Activities

1 Make a large copy of graph **E**. Add the information from graph A to show the main types of jobs on the North Italian Plain.

2 **a)** List six advantages of farming in this region.
 b) Sort the advantages under the headings **Physical** and **Human**.

3 **a)** Name four important industries in this region.

b) Give three reasons why this is the most important region for industry in Italy.
c) Draw a star diagram to show some of the problems which have resulted from industrial growth.

Summary

The North Italian Plain is the richest region in Italy. Most of the land is either used for large towns and industry or for commercial farming.

Life in the South of Italy

The South of Italy is the poorest region in Italy. One area has the lowest standard of living in the EU. Most people still live in hilltop villages in rural areas (photo **B**). The few towns, which are on the coast, have little industry to attract people. Many people from the South have had to migrate either to the North of Italy, to other EU countries or even to North America or Australia to find work. Recently even poorer people from south-east Europe and developing countries have moved into this region.

Land use and jobs

Agriculture is still the major type of land use and 25 in 100 workers are farmers (graph **A**). Most farms are very small. The fields are often spread out and are a long way from the village where the farmer lives. Farming is at a **subsistence** level which means that farmers grow just enough food for their own needs and have very little left over to sell (photo **C**). Vines, olives and fruit are grown on the hillsides beneath the village. Wheat is grown where the land is flatter. Sheep and goats graze on the higher and steeper slopes.

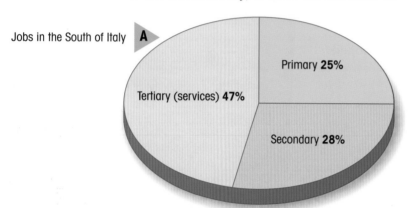

Jobs in the South of Italy **A**

Primary 25%

Tertiary (services) 47%

Secondary 28%

B Disadvantages of farming in the South

Much of the land is high and steep

Little soil on hills due to erosion

Few big banks from which to borrow money

Few farmers own their own land

Little money to buy fertiliser

Far away from urban markets in northern Italy and north-west Europe

Most rain falls in winter. There is a summer drought

Rivers often dry up in summer. Often there is not enough money or water for irrigation schemes

Few local colleges, which means that farming methods are still traditional

Animals are often used instead of modern machinery

Industry

The South of Italy has never been an important industrial region. It is isolated from the rest of Europe by poor transport links. The area has very few natural resources, little money and limited skills. The high birth rate means there are too many people looking for few available jobs. Large numbers, therefore, have had to leave the region in order to find work.

Attempts have been made to improve roads and to introduce new industries. This has only been partly successful as the few new industries, such a steelmaking, chemicals and car assembling, have only benefited a few places (map **D**). Also, as these industries are highly mechanised they do not need to employ many people.

Despite these problems the South is slowly becoming better off. Marshy areas have been drained and trees planted. New dams, irrigation schemes and motorways have been built. The hot, dry summers and sandy beaches are attracting more tourists. Some of the earlier migrants to the North have returned with the money which they earned there. Even so, the gap in wealth between the North and the South of Italy continues to grow.

C The South of Italy

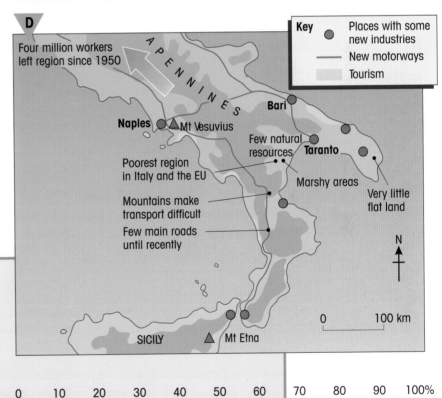

D

Four million workers left region since 1950

APENNINES

Naples ● ▲ Mt Vesuvius

Bari

Few natural resources

Taranto

Poorest region in Italy and the EU

Marshy areas

Mountains make transport difficult

Very little flat land

Few main roads until recently

SICILY   ▲ Mt Etna

N

0   100 km

Key
● Places with some new industries
— New motorways
Tourism

Activities

1 Make a large copy of graph **E**. Add the information from graph **A** to show the main types of jobs in the South of Italy.

2 **a)** List six problems facing the farmers in this region.
   b) Sort these problems under the headings **Physical** and **Human**.

3 **a)** Name three important industries in this region.
   b) Give three reasons why this area has had difficulty in attracting industry.
   c) Draw a star diagram to show some of the recent improvements made in this region.

E

0	10	20	30	40	50	60	70	80	90	100%

Summary

The South of Italy is the poorest region in the country. Most of the land is used for subsistence farming and some for industry and tourism. Large areas have very limited use for people.

Location and . . .

All three countries are found north of the Equator, mainly between the Tropic of Cancer and the Arctic Circle (map **A**).

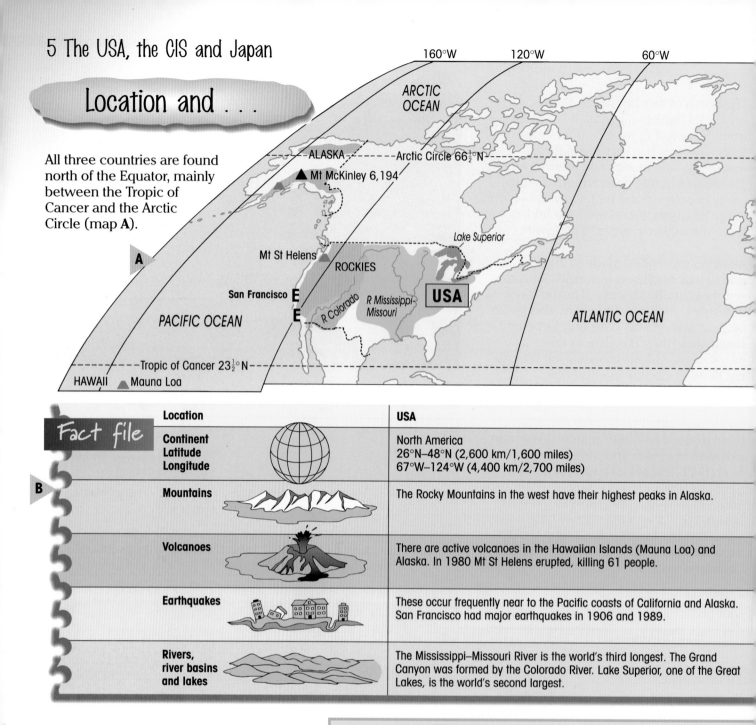

A

160°W 120°W 60°W

ARCTIC OCEAN

ALASKA —— Arctic Circle 66½°N

▲ Mt McKinley 6,194

Lake Superior

Mt St Helens

ROCKIES

San Francisco **E**

E

R Colorado R Mississippi–Missouri

USA

PACIFIC OCEAN

ATLANTIC OCEAN

—— Tropic of Cancer 23½°N ——

HAWAII ▲ Mauna Loa

Fact file

Location		USA
Continent Latitude Longitude		North America 26°N–48°N (2,600 km/1,600 miles) 67°W–124°W (4,400 km/2,700 miles)
Mountains		The Rocky Mountains in the west have their highest peaks in Alaska.
Volcanoes		There are active volcanoes in the Hawaiian Islands (Mauna Loa) and Alaska. In 1980 Mt St Helens erupted, killing 61 people.
Earthquakes		These occur frequently near to the Pacific coasts of California and Alaska. San Francisco had major earthquakes in 1906 and 1989.
Rivers, river basins and lakes		The Mississippi–Missouri River is the world's third longest. The Grand Canyon was formed by the Colorado River. Lake Superior, one of the Great Lakes, is the world's second largest.

B

Physical features

Japan, western USA and the east of the CIS all border the Pacific Ocean. These places have high mountains, active volcanoes and frequent, often severe, earthquakes. The south of the CIS also has high mountains and strong earthquakes. However, most parts of the CIS and the central parts of the USA are low-lying and relatively flat. Both areas have long rivers which meander across wide plains, whereas in Japan rivers are short and fast-flowing.

Activities

1 An aeroplane pilot and a car driver have to cross each of the three countries at their widest point. The pilot can fly at 480 km/hour (300 miles/hour) and the car driver can drive at 80 km/hour (50 miles/hour). Each can travel in a straight line. Using the distances from table **B**, complete table **C**. Times to cross the UK are given for comparison.

C

	Time in hours to cross			
	UK	USA	CIS	Japan
Plane	1			
Car	6			

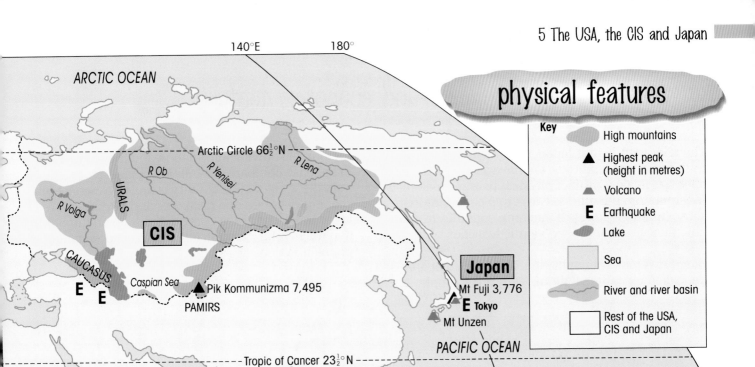

physical features

Key

	High mountains
▲	Highest peak (height in metres)
▲	Volcano
E	Earthquake
	Lake
	Sea
	River and river basin
	Rest of the USA, CIS and Japan

CIS (most of the former USSR)	Japan
Europe and Asia 35°N–74°N (4,900 km/3,000 miles) 22°E–170°W (9,600 km/6,000 miles)	Asia 31°N–46°N (1,600 km/1,000 miles) 130°E–146°E (1,300 km/800 miles)
The highest mountains (Caucasus and Pamirs) are along the southern borders. The Urals divide Europe and Asia. Much of the CIS is low-lying.	Much of the country is mountainous with only 17 per cent being flat enough for farming, industry and settlement.
The only active volcanoes are near to the Pacific Ocean to the north of Japan.	Japan is a group of volcanic islands. It has over 60 active volcanoes. Mt Fuji last erupted in 1708. Mt Unzen killed 34 people in 1991.
The most severe earthquakes occur in the Caucasus where, in 1988, 25,000 people died in Armenia. Other earthquake areas are the southern mountains and near to the Pacific.	Many minor earthquakes occur each year. The most severe destroyed Tokyo and killed over 100,000 people in 1923. The most recent was in Kobe in 1995.
The CIS has many very long, meandering rivers. World ranking – the Ob is the 4th longest river, the Lena 9th, the Yenisei 13th and the Volga 16th. The Caspian Sea is the world's largest lake.	The steep mountains and heavy rain create many short but fast-flowing rivers. Lake Biwa is the largest lake.

2 Solve the clues here by using the information on these two pages. The first letters are given to help you. Sort your answers under the headings **USA**, **CIS**, and **Japan**.

PO	Sea area between USA and Japan	CS	Largest lake in world
MM	Longest river in the USA	O	Longest river in CIS
Mc	Highest mountain in the USA	MSH	Volcano which erupted in 1980
A	25,000 died in this earthquake	SF	City twice hit by earthquakes
F	Highest mountain in Japan	Co	River flowing in Grand Canyon
L	Ninth longest river in the world	B	Largest lake in Japan
T	100,000 died in 1923 earthquake	S	Second largest lake in world
Ca	High mountains in south of CIS	U	Mountains between Europe and Asia
R	High mountains in west of USA	AO	Sea area north of USA and CIS
		V	Longest river in Europe
		ML	Volcano in the Hawaiian Islands

Summary

Each country in the world has its own distinctive physical features making it different from all other countries.

Population and economic features

The USA, the CIS and Japan are three of the world's most important countries. We have already seen how each has its own distinct **physical** features making it different from the others. These two pages compare some **human** features of the three countries to show how they give different economic activities.

Diagram **A** looks at population. The maps that are used are called **topological maps**. They are a simple method of showing information and they help us to make easy comparisons between places. In the first map the area of each country is drawn to scale but its shape is distorted and distances and directions are inaccurate. The size a country is drawn on the other two maps is based upon either its total population or its population density.

A

Area

Look at the first map. By counting the number of squares you can work out the approximate area of each country. Based on area, the CIS is the largest, and the USA the fourth largest country in the world. The UK, which has been added for interest, and Japan, are by comparison very small.

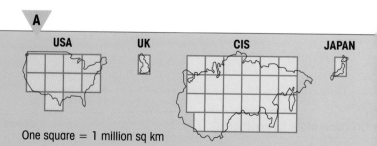

One square = 1 million sq km

Population

When looking at the total population of the four countries, the CIS is still the largest, closely followed by the USA. However, the difference between them is much less than it was when comparing their areas.

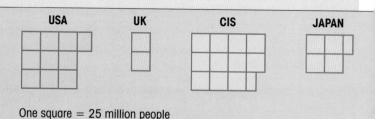

One square = 25 million people

Population density

Population density is a measure of how crowded a place is. The population density for the USA and the CIS is very low, showing that neither is very crowded. The situation in Japan is very different. It has a large population living in a small area. This means that it has a high population density and is very crowded. In fact, as only 17 per cent of Japan is flat enough to live on, parts of the country have over 1,000 people to every square kilometre. This lack of space is one of Japan's biggest problems.

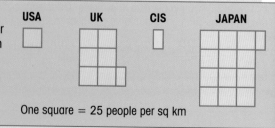

One square = 25 people per sq km

Life expectancy

The USA, the CIS and Japan also have an increasing number of people living to an older age. All four countries shown in the graph have a life expectancy well above the average for the world, with Japan having the highest in the world. In 1988, 12 per cent of Japan's population was aged over 65. Estimates suggest that this will double to 24 per cent by the year 2025. This means that an increasing amount of money will be needed to look after the elderly.

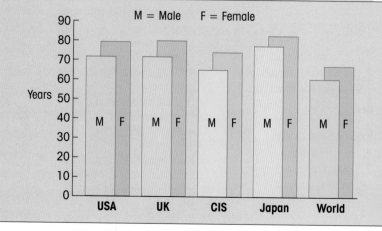

Economic activities and trade

The USA and Japan are very industrialised. They are world leaders in producing high-technology products such as cars and electrical goods. Much of their wealth comes from selling these products to other countries. The CIS is also industrialised but its factories are less modern, and it produces fewer goods to sell than the USA and Japan.

Table **B** uses statistics to summarise the trade of the three countries. It gives information about the main goods sold and bought by each country. Goods sold are called **exports**. Goods bought are called **imports**. It also shows their main trade links.

B

	USA	CIS	Japan
Four main imports (in order)	Machinery Transport Clothing Minerals	Machinery Clothing Foodstuffs Minerals	Oil Minerals Timber Clothing
Value of imports (US $ billions)	520	120	240
Share of world trade	15%	6%	9%
Main trade links	Canada and Mexico 26% Japan 23%, EU 14%	Eastern Europe 23%, EU 18%, Central and South America 6%	USA 39%, South and SE Asia 23%, EU 17%
Four main exports (in order)	Machinery Cars and planes Chemicals Grain (cereals)	Machinery Oil and gas Iron and steel Timber	Cars Electrical goods Telecommunications Machinery
Value of exports (US $ billions)	400	100	300

Activities

1 Make a Fact File like the one below. Use information from diagram **A** to complete it.

Fact file

	USA	CIS	JAPAN
Area (million sq km)			
Population (millions)			
Population density (people per sq km)			
Life expectancy (give male or female)			

2 **a)** Draw a topological map to compare the amounts of world trade for the USA, the CIS and Japan.

Make one square = 1%

b) Under the map for each country:
- give its two main imports
- give its two main exports
- say if it sells more than it buys. (This is the difference between import value and export value.)

EXTRA

Collect adverts for at least ten things made in Japan. Make them into a wall display and add a title.

Summary

The USA, the CIS and Japan all play important roles in the world. Industry and trade have helped to make the USA and Japan wealthy.

What is Japan like?

Japan lies off the east coast of Asia in the Pacific Ocean. It consists of four large islands and over 1,000 smaller ones. The four largest are Honshu – which is a little larger than Great Britain – Hokkaido, Kyushu and Shikoku. The islands were formed by volcanoes, many of which are still active. Most of Japan is mountainous with less than 20 per cent of the country being flat enough for farming or settlement. The climate is very warm in summer. The south of the country has very mild winters but it is much colder in the mountains and the extreme north. All of Japan receives a plentiful supply of rainfall throughout the year. There are several **natural hazards**.

- Volcanic eruptions, the occasional severe earthquake and numerous minor earth tremors.
- **Tsunamis** – huge tidal waves caused by the undersea earthquakes.
- **Typhoons** – very strong hurricane-force winds.
- Heavy winter snowfalls in the north.

Yet despite these hazards the Japanese believe that nature has been kind to them.

- The heavy rainfall has covered the mountains with forest and provides water for irrigation.
- The warm, wet summers are ideal for growing rice.
- Volcanic eruptions give fertile soil.
- The fast-flowing rivers supply fresh water and produce hydro-electricity.
- The warm seas are an important source of food.

Traditional way of life (photos **B** and **C**)

The islands of Japan were sufficiently isolated, until recently, for the Japanese to develop a unique culture and way of life. The Japanese language is not easy to learn and is even harder to write. All Japanese words are written using a system that has 46 symbols. Foreign words are usually written in a second system using 46 different symbols. The traditional dress is a long, loose fitting robe (kimono), a waist

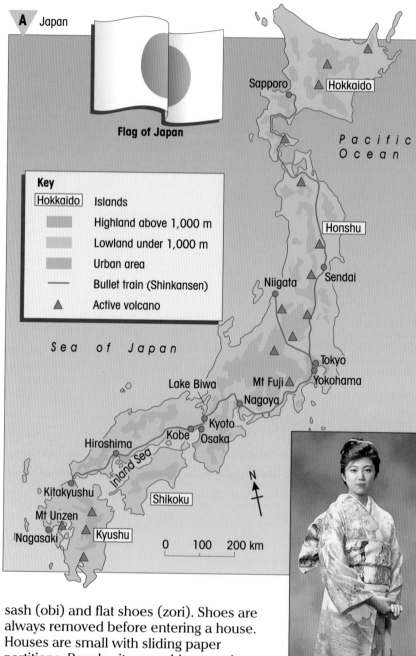

A Japan

Flag of Japan

Key

Hokkaido	Islands
	Highland above 1,000 m
	Lowland under 1,000 m
	Urban area
—	Bullet train (Shinkansen)
▲	Active volcano

Pacific Ocean

Sea of Japan

Sapporo · Hokkaido

Honshu

Niigata · Sendai

Tokyo
Yokohama

Lake Biwa · Mt Fuji
Nagoya

Kyoto
Kobe · Osaka

Hiroshima

Inland Sea

Kitakyushu

Shikoku

Mt Unzen

Nagasaki · Kyushu

N

0   100   200 km

B Girl in traditional Japanese clothes

sash (obi) and flat shoes (zori). Shoes are always removed before entering a house. Houses are small with sliding paper partitions. People sit on cushions on the floor and bedding is stored away during the day. Although most Japanese are not very religious, many combine the two main religions, using Shinto for weddings and Buddhism for funerals. Several Japanese customs have become well known worldwide. These include sumo wrestling, kendo fencing, karate, paper folding (origami), flower arranging (ikebana) and miniature plant growing (bonsai).

C From left, a Buddhist temple, Sumo wrestling

Modern Japan (photos D and E)

The very rapid growth of cities and industry in the last forty years has dramatically altered the Japanese way of life and made Japan rich. Although Japan has less than 3 per cent of the world's population it earns nearly 10 per cent of the world's money. Most houses are small and are built very close together. They are full of modern gadgets yet they keep the characteristics of traditional homes. City centres have huge shopping centres with department stores full of high quality goods, mostly made in Japan. Tall office blocks tower above congested roads. Streets are full of workers and shoppers during the day. In the evening people seek the active nightlife. Most people wear western style dress.

Most Japanese spend long hours at work and have few holidays. They are extremely loyal to their family and place of work. Politeness is basic to their way of life. They are patriotic, highly educated and skilled. Many children go to extra classes at night because exam failure is considered a family disgrace. Over 90 per cent of children over the age of 16 stay on at school and one third go on to university.

D Tokyo city centre

E Tokyo

F

| Volcanoes _____ | Fast flowing rivers _____ | Warm seas _____ |
| Heavy rain_____ | **How nature helps the Japanese** | Warm, wet summers ___ |

Activities

1 Copy diagram **F**. Add a sentence to each box to show how the Japanese believe nature has been kind to them.

2 Make a wall display to show aspects of Japanese life. You could include language, dress, religion, sport, customs, food and drink.

Summary The lives of people living in Japan are influenced by the physical environment. Living on a group of islands, the Japanese have developed a distinctive culture and way of life.

What are Japan's sources of energy?

Since 1945, Japan has become a major industrial country. By 1990 it had even overtaken the USA as the world's richest nation. Industry, and the transport system to keep it going, use a lot of energy (diagram **A**). What makes Japan's achievements even greater is the fact that the country has very limited energy resources of its own. Japan has used up almost all of its coal reserves and has virtually no oil, natural gas or uranium. Although it has some renewable types of energy, over 80 per cent of Japan's total supplies have to be imported. Graph **B** shows the types of energy which make up Japan's present day supply of electricity.

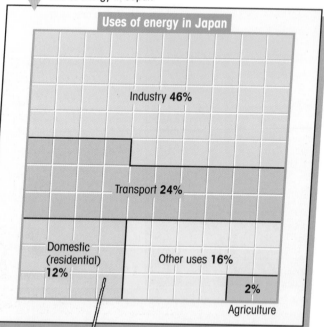

A Use of energy in Japan

Uses of energy in Japan

Industry 46%

Transport 24%

Domestic (residential) 12%

Other uses 16%

2% Agriculture

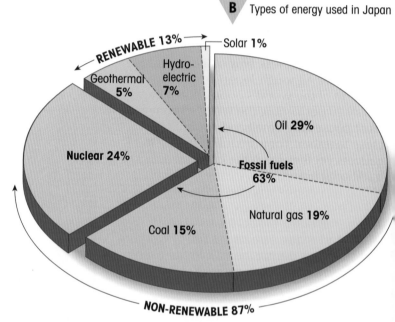

B Types of energy used in Japan

RENEWABLE 13%

Solar 1%

Geothermal 5%

Hydro-electric 7%

Nuclear 24%

Oil 29%

Fossil fuels 63%

Natural gas 19%

Coal 15%

NON-RENEWABLE 87%

Sources of energy within Japan

Coal is mined in Hokkaido and north-west Kyushu. However, it is of poor quality for producing electricity, it is found deep underground and it is dangerous and expensive to mine. In 1960 there were 600 coalmines with 230,000 miners. By 1990 there were only seven coalmines and 20,000 miners. Oil and natural gas are found but in very small amounts.

Hydro-electric power is obtained from Japan's fast-flowing rivers. The largest scheme is on the Kurobe River (map **C**). Water is stored behind a 200 metre high dam before being fed through a series of tunnels cut through the surrounding mountains. Although hydro-electric power only provides 7 per cent of Japan's energy, it has been very important in developing the country's industries.

Japan has the opportunity of developing renewable forms of energy. It already uses **geothermal** heat from several volcanic areas. Strong winds over the land and large waves at sea may be used in the future. However, the cloudy, wet climate reduces the possibility of using **solar** power.

Japan is the world's fourth largest producer of **nuclear** power. Nuclear power already provides over 20 per cent of the country's energy and this could increase next century to over 50 per cent. The Japanese people are very sensitive to the risk of nuclear accidents and there is a growing opposition to the building of more power stations. At present they see little alternative if they are to continue to industrialise and reduce the cost of importing the **fossil fuels** of coal, oil and natural gas.

Sources of energy outside Japan

Japan's rapid industrial growth was based on the import of cheap oil. Most of this oil came from the Middle East. As the world price of oil and as political problems in the Middle East have both increased, then Japan has had to turn more to coal and natural gas. The sources of these types of energy are shown on map **C**.

The Japanese have built large tankers to import oil, coal and natural gas (photo **D**). These tankers use ports in the south and east of the country as these natural harbours are deep and sheltered from typhoons and tsunamis. These ports were places where most Japanese already lived and worked. As nuclear power stations need large amounts of water for cooling purposes they too have been built next to the sea, but on coasts where fewer people live.

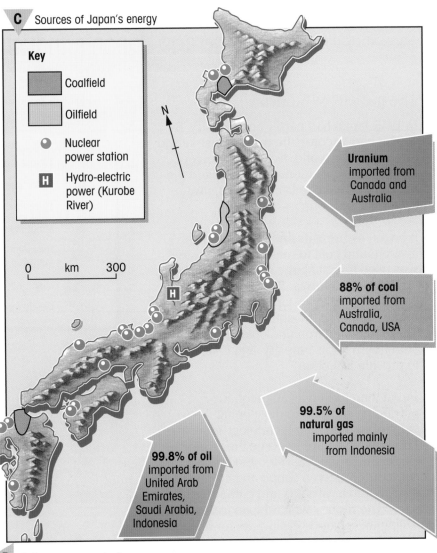

C Sources of Japan's energy

Key

- Coalfield
- Oilfield
- Nuclear power station
- H Hydro-electric power (Kurobe River)

N

0   km   300

Uranium imported from Canada and Australia

88% of coal imported from Australia, Canada, USA

99.5% of natural gas imported mainly from Indonesia

99.8% of oil imported from United Arab Emirates, Saudi Arabia, Indonesia

D A Japanese supertanker

Activities

1 **a)** Draw a pie graph to show the uses of energy in Japan.
   b) Draw a percentage bar graph to show the types of energy used in Japan (see pages 65 and 67).

2 Make a larger copy of table **E**. Complete the table by following the instructions on the right. The figure before each instruction refers to the columns.

1 List the seven types of energy used by Japan. Put them in rank order, the highest first.

2 For each type of energy say if it is renewable, fossil fuel or neither.

3 Put a tick for those types of energy which Japan can mainly provide for itself.

4 Put a tick for those types of energy which Japan has to get from other countries.

5 Write in the names of those countries from which Japan gets the type of energy which you ticked in column 4 (refer to map **C**).

Summary

Japan produces some of its own energy by using hydro, nuclear and geothermal power. However, it is dependent on other countries to supply most of its energy needs.

E

1 Types of energy (in order)	2 Renewable energy, fossil fuel or neither	3 Is it provided by Japan?	4 Is it obtained from another country?	5 Countries from which energy is obtained

Where is Japan's industry located?

The growth of industry

In 1945 Japan had hardly any industry. By 1990 it had become the most industrialised country in the world. How did it achieve this success considering that it lacked the basic industrial needs of flat land, raw materials and sources of energy?

It began by using its limited amounts of iron ore and coal to make steel. The steel was used to build large ships, new factories and houses. The ships were designed to carry to Japan those raw materials which the country needed. These included iron ore, coking coal and aluminium for its industry, and coal and oil to provide its energy.

Japan then turned its attention to producing cars and to developing electronics and high-technology industries. The Japanese have become the world leaders in producing video recorders and camcorders, stereo sound and compact disc systems, cameras and computer parts. The money which Japan makes by selling these goods easily pays for the cost of buying the raw materials and foodstuffs.

The location of industry – sources of energy

Industry needs energy. Japan's early iron and steel works were built in the north of the country where there were supplies of coal for energy, and iron ore (map **A**). As these supplies have been used up then present day industry has chosen sites in the south and east of the country. Compare map **A** on this page with map **C** on the previous page. This shows a link between industrial location and sources of energy in that the main industrial areas lie along the Pacific coast of Japan where large ports import the needed energy supplies; there is a smaller industrial area along the west coast where there are many nuclear and hydro-electric power stations.

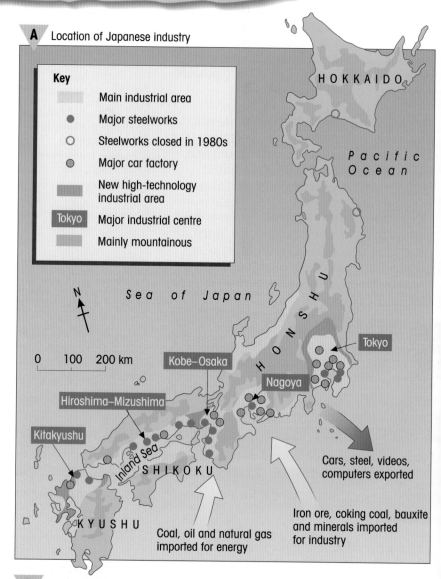

A Location of Japanese industry

Key

- Main industrial area
- ● Major steelworks
- ○ Steelworks closed in 1980s
- ● Major car factory
- New high-technology industrial area
- Tokyo Major industrial centre
- Mainly mountainous

HOKKAIDO

Pacific Ocean

Sea of Japan

HONSHU

Tokyo

Kobe–Osaka

Nagoya

Hiroshima–Mizushima

Kitakyushu

Inland Sea

SHIKOKU

KYUSHU

Cars, steel, videos, computers exported

Coal, oil and natural gas imported for energy

Iron ore, coking coal, bauxite and minerals imported for industry

N

0   100   200 km

B Modern industry in Japan – robots making cars

Other location factors

Diagram **C** gives other reasons why Japan's main industrial regions should be located in the south and east of the country. The Japanese themselves consider the two most important things in finding the site for a new industry to be the distribution of lowland and people, and the location of sheltered deepwater ports. There is now such a shortage of building space that land for any new large factory has to be reclaimed from the sea (photo **D**).

C

s easier to export our cars d electrical goods if they e made near the main ports.

Our industries need a large and rich local market. It is best if they are located near to where most people live.

As we have to import so much fuel (for energy) and raw materials it is best to have industry near to the ports.

e have many deep, eltered harbours hich make ideal ports r big ships.

We have a highly skilled, educated and hardworking workforce.

The best places for motorways and the bullet train are in the south and east.

We have very little flat land where we can build factories.

Activities

1 Write out the sentences below in the correct order to describe the growth of industry in Japan.

◆ Ships and factories were built using steel.
◆ Car and electrical industries developed.
◆ Steel was first made from local raw materials.
◆ Money earned from selling goods was spent on buying raw materials.
◆ Ships were used to import raw materials.

2 Make a simple sketch of the car factory shown in photo **D**. Add the following labels to show why it was a good site to locate a large modern car factory.

◆ Large local market for cars
◆ Good accessibility by motorway
◆ Flat land reclaimed from sea
◆ Deep and sheltered harbour
◆ Port to import raw materials and energy
◆ Port to export finished cars
◆ Attractive location with hills and coast

D Mazda car factory, Hiroshima

Summary

Although some industry in Japan is built near to sources of energy, the most important location factors are the distribution of lowland and people, and the position of sheltered deepwater ports.

77

How has industry affected the environment?

With so little flat land in Japan there is competition for space for industry, housing, transport, recreation and farming. The growth of cities and industry, and the development of transport have created a number of environmental problems. These problems include the loss of land for farming, the removal of forests and the destruction of natural habitats, as well as increasing air and water pollution.

Farming

Land use in Japan shows that only 14 per cent of the country is used for farming.

Land use	Percentage
Arable (growing crops)	12
Pastoral (grass for farm animals)	2
Urban (houses, industry and transport)	3
Forest	67
Others (mainly mountains and lakes)	16

Most Japanese farms and their fields are very small. The average farm size of 1.1 hectares is about the same as two football pitches. Each farm has to be carefully looked after and no land is wasted. This is called **intensive** farming. Even so, farmers are finding it harder and harder to earn a living as more of their land is being taken over for housing and by industry. Japanese farmers have had to change their methods of farming in order to survive. Three of these changes are shown in photos **A**, **B** and **C**.

A

Small, flat terraces have been built on hillsides to allow more crops, usually rice, to grow. Each terrace is surrounded by an earth wall. This wall traps rainwater for the crops and reduces the amount of soil being washed downhill.

B Many vegetable crops are grown under vinyl sheets or in vinyl greenhouses. Crops grow and ripen more quickly. This allows two or three crops to be grown each year.

C Labour-saving machines have been designed to work on small farms. Most farmers own a power cultivator (their fields are too small for tractors), a rice planter, a rice harvester and sprayers.

Natural habitats

Although two thirds of Japan is still covered in forest, much of this is either in mountainous areas or has been replanted. In lowland areas there is very little natural vegetation left and this has meant a loss of wildlife **habitats**. As a result many species of wildlife – animals, birds and plants – have become either extinct or endangered. To try to protect their environment the Japanese have set up many National Parks (photo **D**).

Wider environmental problems

In developing their own industries and more recently in trying to protect their own forests and wildlife habitats, the Japanese have been accused of spoiling environments elsewhere in the world. Some of these accusations, together with the Japanese reply, are given in diagram **E**.

D Mount Fuji National Park

E

We come from South-east Asia. You are rapidly cutting down our forests to supply your own needs for timber and paper. You buy our raw materials. We grow crops for you instead of trying to feed ourselves.

You can plant more trees. You do not need your raw materials as you have so little industry. You have to sell some of your crops to us so that you can buy our goods.

You have endangered whales and, by using large drift nets, dolphins. You have also imported lots of ivory.

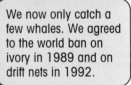

We now only catch a few whales. We agreed to the world ban on ivory in 1989 and on drift nets in 1992.

Activities

1 You are a farmer in Japan. Write to a friend in Britain describing how you have had to change your farming methods. Your letter should be about half a page in length and should include the terms 'small flat terraces', 'vinyl sheets' and 'labour-saving machines'.

2 Which of the two opinions given in sketch **E** do you consider to be the more important? Give reasons for your answer.

E X T R A

Design a poster to advertise Mount Fuji National Park. Use photo **D** to help you to:
a) describe the different natural habitats
b) suggest activities which visitors to the park might do
c) show an attractive scene of the park.

Summary

The growth of industry has resulted in the loss of farmland and wildlife habitats. This has led to changes in farming methods and the creation of National Parks.

Is Japan's environment still at risk?

A Face mask worn to reduce danger from air pollution – Tokyo, 1970s

The environment in 1980

As Japan developed its industries it gave little thought as to how this would affect the environment. Water supplies and the air became severely polluted. This caused serious health problems to people and threatened the existence of wildlife.

The worst areas were found around the coastal areas of Tokyo Bay and the Inland Sea. These places had high population densities, many large industries and thermal power stations and an increasing number of cars.

Diagram **B** includes a Landsat photo of Tokyo Bay and gives the major causes of air and water pollution in that area.

B Causes of pollution in and around Tokyo Bay, 1980

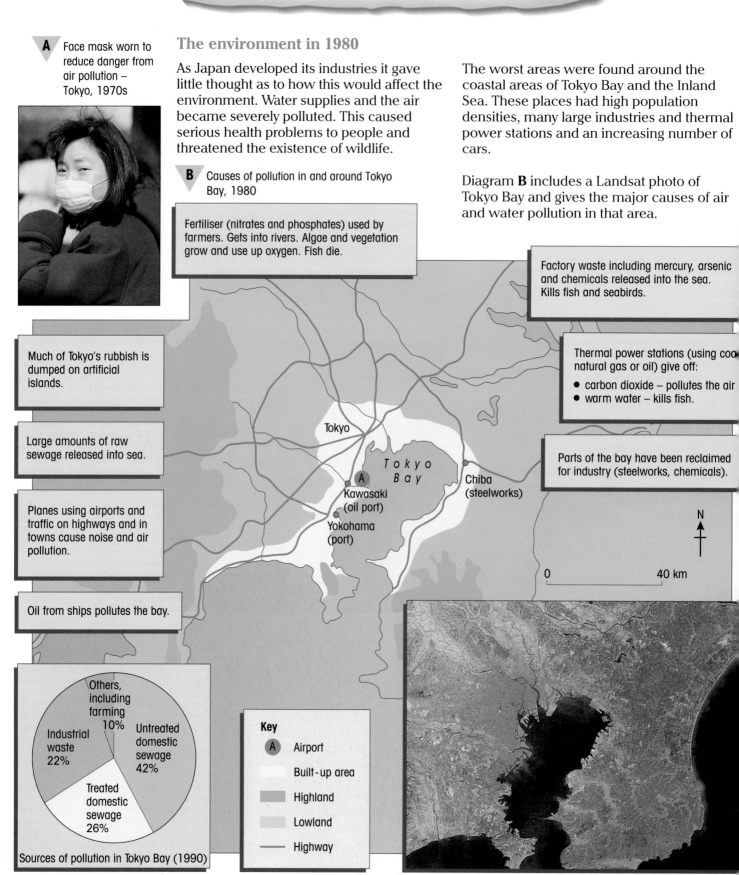

Fertiliser (nitrates and phosphates) used by farmers. Gets into rivers. Algae and vegetation grow and use up oxygen. Fish die.

Factory waste including mercury, arsenic and chemicals released into the sea. Kills fish and seabirds.

Much of Tokyo's rubbish is dumped on artificial islands.

Thermal power stations (using coal, natural gas or oil) give off:
- carbon dioxide – pollutes the air
- warm water – kills fish.

Large amounts of raw sewage released into sea.

Parts of the bay have been reclaimed for industry (steelworks, chemicals).

Planes using airports and traffic on highways and in towns cause noise and air pollution.

Oil from ships pollutes the bay.

Tokyo

Tokyo Bay

A Kawasaki (oil port)

Yokohama (port)

Chiba (steelworks)

N

0 — 40 km

Key
- A Airport
- Built-up area
- Highland
- Lowland
- Highway

Sources of pollution in Tokyo Bay (1990):
- Others, including farming 10%
- Industrial waste 22%
- Untreated domestic sewage 42%
- Treated domestic sewage 26%

The environment today

In the early 1970s, the Japanese government produced standards for the quality of the environment. These standards were aimed at controlling levels of air, water and noise pollution. Japan was then faced with the same problem as the other rich industrial countries. Should it use its money and technology to reduce environmental pollution or to develop new industries and become even richer? Japan claims it has done more than other industrial countries to control pollution. Poor countries claim that Japan has still not done very much.

What has been done? The quality of the air has certainly improved. All cars use unleaded petrol. There are strict rules reducing the release of car exhaust fumes and factory gases. Smog-related illnesses have decreased and people rarely have to use smog masks. Moss, which quickly dies in polluted air, is again growing in Tokyo's parks. Although most Japanese dislike the increase in nuclear power it has reduced the amount of carbon dioxide (CO_2) released into the air. Japan releases less CO_2 per person than most other industrial countries but far more than the poorer countries (graph **C**). The Japanese are only slowly managing to improve the quality of water in rivers and the sea. Industry is releasing less waste and more domestic sewage is being treated before it enters the sea. Unfortunately the pollution of earlier years cannot be cleaned up overnight.

Activities

1 Using diagram **B**:
  a) Draw a star diagram to show eight types of pollution affecting Tokyo Bay.
  b) Give the causes and effects of any four of these types of pollution.

2 Look at graph **C**.
  a) In which year was Japan's pollution problem greatest?
  b) Which types of pollution are less today than they were in the 1960s?
  c) Why have levels of rural water pollution shown a slight rise? (*Clue* – farming page 78)

3 **a)** Describe three things which have helped to reduce pollution in Japan.
  b) Give two effects of improved air quality.

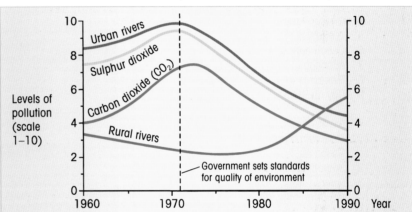

C Types of pollution in Japan

EXTRA

Look at graph **D** which shows carbon dioxide (CO_2) pollution as a world problem.
  a) Which two countries give off most CO_2?
  b) How much CO_2 does Japan give off?
  c) Explain why poor countries like Kenya and India cause less CO_2 pollution than rich countries.
  d) Why is it important for the world to reduce CO_2 pollution?

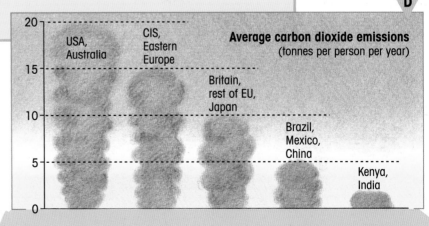

D

Average carbon dioxide emissions (tonnes per person per year)

Summary The rapid growth of industry in Japan caused air and water pollution. The task of cleaning up the environment will take a long time and is costing a lot of money.

6 World development

Where in the world ...?

Activities

1 The world's largest cities and longest rivers are marked on the map. See if you can find them.

2 Complete the crossword by solving the following clues. All of the answers can be found on these two pages.

Across

1 South America's highest mountain
2 A mountain in Africa
3 South American city
4 River in Africa
5 World's highest mountain
6 Ocean east of Africa
7 Aconcagua is in these mountains
8 Everest is in these mountains
9 City on the River Yangtse

Down

1 South American river
10 Mountain range - SCIORKE
11 Ocean east of America
12 Sometimes called Antarctic Ocean
13 River in North America
14 Important city in USA
15 Russia's capital city
16 City on River Nile

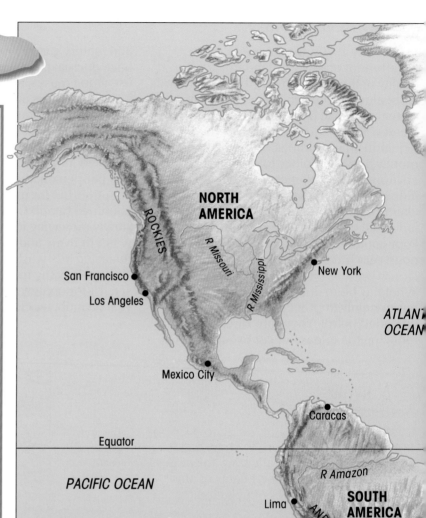

NORTH AMERICA

ROCKIES

R Missouri

R Mississippi

San Francisco

Los Angeles

New York

ATLANTIC OCEAN

Mexico City

Caracas

Equator

PACIFIC OCEAN

R Amazon

Lima

ANDES

SOUTH AMERICA

Rio de Ja

Sao Paulo

Buenos Aires

World's largest cities (estimates 2000)		
City	Country	Population in millions
Mexico City	Mexico	25.6
São Paulo	Brazil	22.1
Tokyo	Japan	19.0
Shanghai	China	17.0
New York	USA	16.8
Calcutta	India	15.7
Bombay	India	15.4
Beijing	China	14.0
Los Angeles	USA	13.9
Jakarta	Indonesia	13.7

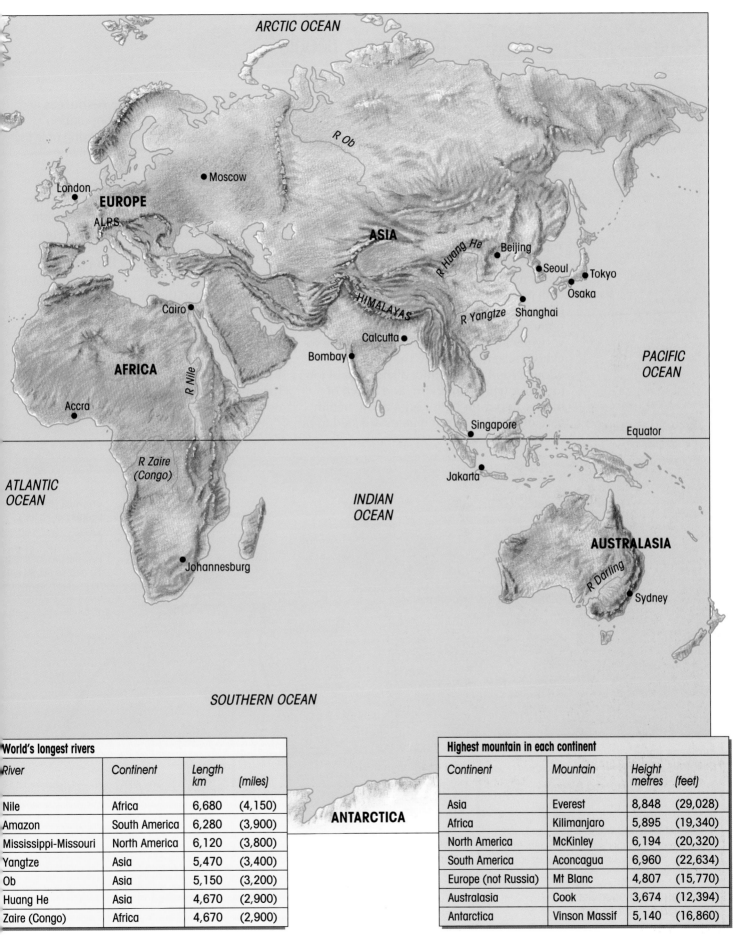

World's longest rivers

River	Continent	Length km	(miles)
Nile	Africa	6,680	(4,150)
Amazon	South America	6,280	(3,900)
Mississippi-Missouri	North America	6,120	(3,800)
Yangtze	Asia	5,470	(3,400)
Ob	Asia	5,150	(3,200)
Huang He	Asia	4,670	(2,900)
Zaire (Congo)	Africa	4,670	(2,900)

Highest mountain in each continent

Continent	Mountain	Height metres	(feet)
Asia	Everest	8,848	(29,028)
Africa	Kilimanjaro	5,895	(19,340)
North America	McKinley	6,194	(20,320)
South America	Aconcagua	6,960	(22,634)
Europe (not Russia)	Mt Blanc	4,807	(15,770)
Australasia	Cook	3,674	(12,394)
Antarctica	Vinson Massif	5,140	(16,860)

Too many people?

This unit is about **development**. Development is about making life better for people. It is about improving the important things in people's lives such as their health, food, housing and education. Improving these things helps people to have higher **living standards** and a better **quality of life**.

You have already learnt that some places are less developed than others. There are many reasons for this. One of them is to do with population. As map **A** shows, some places in the world are very crowded. If the population of these places is also growing very quickly it can be difficult to provide for everyone's needs. There may not be enough food to go round, a shortage of jobs for those who want them, and a lack of money to pay for better education, health care or housing. These places are said to be **overpopulated**.

Overpopulation is when the **resources** of an area cannot support the population living there. The result is a lowering of living standards and a poorer quality of life.

To help development and improve living standards, some countries make efforts to limit population growth by reducing birth rates. To do this they try to persuade people that small families can be healthier, better fed, wealthier and happier than large families. China, the world's most populated country, has had the most success in controlling population growth. Here a mixture of education, benefits and strict laws in the 1980s helped them towards their aim of **one-child families**. Unfortunately, birth control programmes have not been so successful in other countries.

A World population distribution

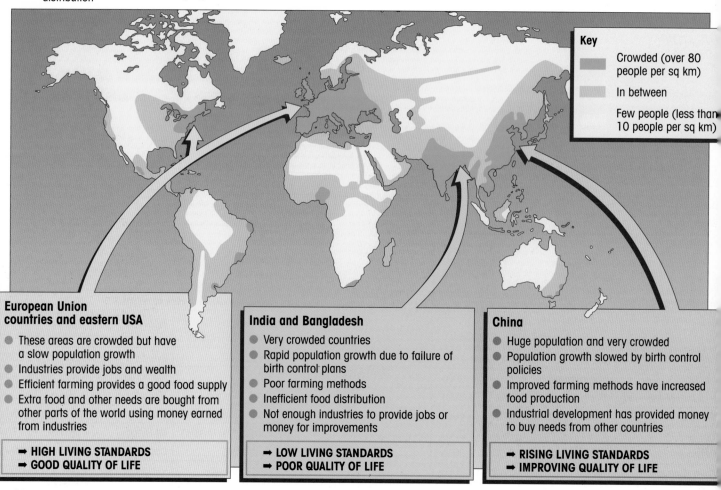

Key

■ Crowded (over 80 people per sq km)

■ In between

□ Few people (less than 10 people per sq km)

European Union countries and eastern USA

- These areas are crowded but have a slow population growth
- Industries provide jobs and wealth
- Efficient farming provides a good food supply
- Extra food and other needs are bought from other parts of the world using money earned from industries

➡ HIGH LIVING STANDARDS
➡ GOOD QUALITY OF LIFE

India and Bangladesh

- Very crowded countries
- Rapid population growth due to failure of birth control plans
- Poor farming methods
- Inefficient food distribution
- Not enough industries to provide jobs or money for improvements

➡ LOW LIVING STANDARDS
➡ POOR QUALITY OF LIFE

China

- Huge population and very crowded
- Population growth slowed by birth control policies
- Improved farming methods have increased food production
- Industrial development has provided money to buy needs from other countries

➡ RISING LIVING STANDARDS
➡ IMPROVING QUALITY OF LIFE

B India – why so many children?

There is a lot of work to do here. We need our children to help us.

Life can be very hard here. We never stop working yet we're always short of food, and our living conditions never seem to get any better.

Having a big family increases my importance in the village.

We need children to look after us when we are old and cannot work

Birth control is against my religion

We need many children because so many die from diseases

C China – why the one-child family?

Because we have only one child, our government gives us free education, better housing and extra money. They also give us a pension when we get old.

We work hard in China but a small family is easier to look after and our quality of life is much better than it used to be.

Families all help each other here. There's no real need for lots of children.

We have a good health care system in China. Very few children die of diseases.

Activities

1 Look at cartoon **D**. Imagine that the number of people in your classroom was suddenly doubled or even trebled.
 a) What problems would it cause?
 b) What shortages would there be?
 c) How would it affect your learning?

2 a) Write out the meaning of **overpopulation**.
 b) Give three problems that may result from overpopulation in a country like India.

D

3 Look at sketches **B** and **C** which give some reasons for population size in India and China. Copy and complete table **E** by putting a tick or a cross in each box.

E

	India	China
Children needed to do work		
Children needed for old age		
Pension scheme for old age		
Good health care		
Disease problems		
Large families		
Improved conditions		
Only slow improvement		

4 What are the advantages of having small families?

E X T R A

Explain how crowded places like the European Union and eastern USA have high living standards and a good quality of life.

Summary

Some countries are crowded and have a rapid population growth. This can cause problems for people and slow down development.

How do jobs affect development?

The jobs people do can be divided into three different types. These are **primary**, **secondary** and **tertiary**. The number of people working in these different types of job varies from place to place and changes with time.

The proportion of the population working in primary, secondary or tertiary jobs in any place is called the **employment structure**. The diagram below shows how the employment structure changes as a country develops.

A

Our country is in the early stages of development. We are still poor and have low living standards. Most of our labour force works in **primary** industries like farming and mining. Farming is important to us because we have to produce enough food for our own people. To improve our living standards we need to buy goods and machinery from rich countries. Selling primary products like iron ore and timber helps us pay for these things.

Our country is beginning to develop. We now have many factories and most of our people work in **secondary** industries. We still produce most of our own food but the use of machines has reduced the number of people who have to work on farms. We are now much richer than before and our transport systems, health care and education have all improved. This is leading to an increase in **tertiary** (service) industry jobs.

We live in one of the more developed countries. Many of our people are employed in **tertiary** industries. These people provide a service. They work in places like hospitals, schools, offices, banks, shops and the entertainment industry. We still have many secondary industries but they need fewer workers because we use machines, robots and computers in our factories. We have very few people working in primary industries because we are rich enough to buy most of our primary goods from other countries.

Map **B** shows some differences in employment structures. These are constantly changing, however . For example, 200 years ago the UK had an employment structure similar to that of present-day India.

Since then changes in farming methods and the growth of manufacturing industries and services have altered that structure. The UK is now one of the world's more developed countries.

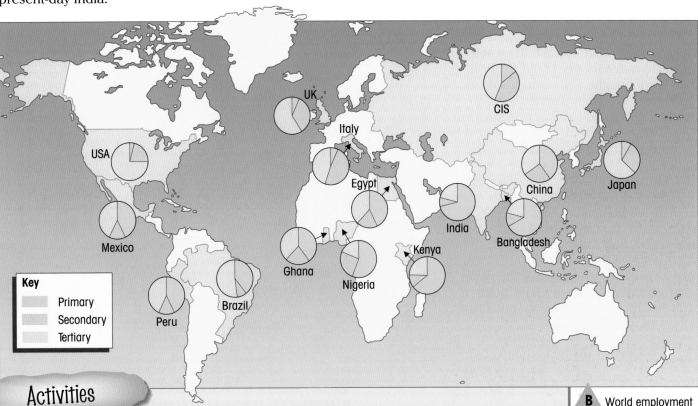

Key
- Primary
- Secondary
- Tertiary

B World employment structures

Activities

1 Give the meaning of the term **employment structure**.

2 Four of the following six statements are correct. Write out the correct ones.
- Employment structures are the same everywhere.
- Employment structures vary from place to place.
- Employment structures change from time to time.
- Poor countries have few workers in primary industries.
- Poor countries have many workers in primary industries.
- Rich countries have few workers in primary industries.

3 Using map **B**:
   a) Name the four most developed countries (those with very few primary jobs).
   b) Name the eight least developed countries (those with a lot of primary jobs).

4 Table **C** shows job types in Britain for 1790, 1890 and 1990.
   a) Draw three pie charts to show the information. Use the same colours as those on map **B** and add a key.
   b) Label each of the pie charts with one of the following:
      - A more developed stage
      - Beginning to develop
      - Early stages of development.
   c) Describe the changes shown by the pie charts.

C

Year	Primary (%)	Secondary (%)	Tertiary (%)
1790	75	15	10
1890	4	56	40
1990	3	32	65

E X T R A

Describe and give reasons for the living standards that are likely in:
- Bangladesh and Kenya
- Italy and Japan.

Summary

There is a link between the employment structure of a country and its level of development. Poor countries have a larger primary workforce than rich countries.

How does trade affect development?

No country has everything that it wants. All countries have to buy from and sell to each other. They **buy** things that they need or would like to have. They **sell** things to make money to pay for what they have bought. The exchanging of goods and materials like this is called **trade**. Goods sold to other countries are called **exports**. Goods that are bought by a country are called **imports**.

Unfortunately not all countries get a fair deal from world trade. As diagram **A** shows, the richer countries of the North earn much more from trading than the poorer countries of the South. One reason for this is that the poorer countries mainly export **primary goods** while the richer countries mainly export **manufactured goods**. The prices of primary goods are low compared with those of manufactured goods. The poorer countries therefore make much less

money from their trade than the richer countries. This unfair trade is a main reason why poor countries remain poor.

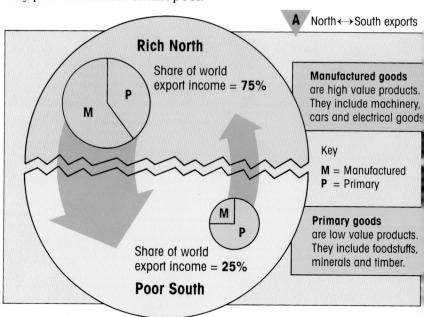

A North↔South exports

Rich North

Share of world export income = **75%**

P

M

Manufactured goods are high value products. They include machinery, cars and electrical goods

Key

M = Manufactured
P = Primary

M
P

Share of world export income = **25%**

Poor South

Primary goods are low value products. They include foodstuffs, minerals and timber.

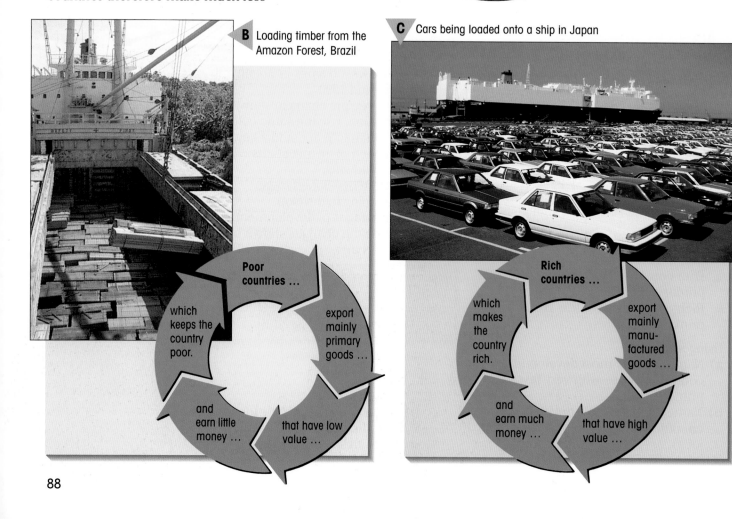

B Loading timber from the Amazon Forest, Brazil

C Cars being loaded onto a ship in Japan

Poor countries ...

which keeps the country poor.

export mainly primary goods ...

and earn little money ...

that have low value ...

Rich countries ...

which makes the country rich.

export mainly manufactured goods ...

and earn much money ...

that have high value ...

Diagram **D** shows another problem faced by developing countries. Many of them rely heavily on just one major export. Ghana, for example, earns 80 per cent of its income from selling cocoa. If there is a good crop and the price for cocoa is high then Ghana will prosper. If, however, the crop fails or the price in the world market falls, the country may struggle to survive because it is so dependent on that one export.

There have been many attempts to keep the prices of primary goods high to try to protect countries like Ghana. Oil-producing countries, for example, have joined together and successfully controlled oil prices. Nigeria and Egypt are countries that have benefited from this success. Unfortunately most other attempts to control prices have failed.

D Single export countries

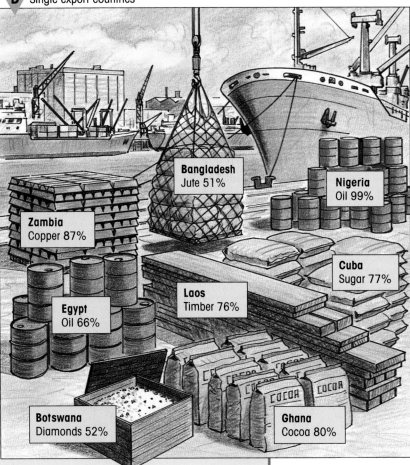

Zambia Copper 87%

Bangladesh Jute 51%

Nigeria Oil 99%

Cuba Sugar 77%

Egypt Oil 66%

Laos Timber 76%

Botswana Diamonds 52%

Ghana Cocoa 80%

Activities

1 a) Make a copy of table **E**.

E

Country	GDP	Primary exports	Manufactured exports

b) List the eight countries from **F** in order of their wealth.
(Highest GDP first)
c) List the exports of each country in either the **Primary** or **Manufactured** columns.
d) Shade lightly in yellow the less developed countries.
(GDP less than US$ 3,000)
e) Write a sentence to describe what your table shows about the exports of:
● the more developed countries
● the less developed countries.

F

Country	GNP 1993 (US $/person)	Main exports
Brazil	3,020	Coffee, machinery, meat
Egypt	660	Oil, fruit, vegetables
Ghana	430	Cocoa, aluminium, timber
Italy	19,620	Machinery, clothing
Japan	31,450	Electrical goods, cars
Kenya	270	Coffee, tea
UK	17,970	Machinery, chemicals
USA	24,750	Machinery, chemicals

G

2 a) From diagram **D** name the countries that depend on one product for:
● over three-quarters of their exports
● between half and three-quarters of their exports.
b) Why do countries that depend mainly on one export often have money problems?

3 Make a larger copy of diagram **G** and add the following information to the correct boxes.
● Crop failure
● Loss of income
● Decline in living standards
● Reliance on one main export
● Fall in price

Summary

Trade is important in the world because it helps countries share resources and earn money. Rich countries gain more from trading than poor countries.

How can the rich help the poor?

One way to help countries develop and improve their living standards is to give them **aid**. Aid is a form of help. It is a practical way for wealthy countries to help poorer countries. It can be given in two main ways.

- The first is as **short-term aid**. Short-term aid helps solve immediate problems. It brings help quickly to people affected by diasters and emergencies. Floods, earthquakes, volcanic eruptions, famine and even wars are some of the events that bring about a need for short-term aid.
- The second is **long-term aid**. The aim of this type of aid is to improve basic living standards and enable people to make better use of their own resources. Long-term aid should help a country progress and improve its overall level of development.

Aid can be given in many different ways. Some of these are shown in diagram **A**.

Giving help to others can bring many benefits but it can also cause problems. Some aid projects, for example, are so large that they damage the environment and are too big and complicated for local people to manage. The Aswan Dam in Egypt is one such example. Others cause people to change their lives too much and spoil the traditions of the area. Some forms of aid even fail to reach the people for whom they were intended. In Somalia, for example, some of the food aid sent there never reached the millions of people who were dying of starvation. This was partly due to a lack of transport but also because of civil war in the country.

Great care has to be taken in providing countries with the right kind of aid. A well thought out and carefully planned programme can help to provide the building blocks for a country's future. Cartoon **B** shows the kind of aid which is most likely to bring benefits to a country and help its poorest people.

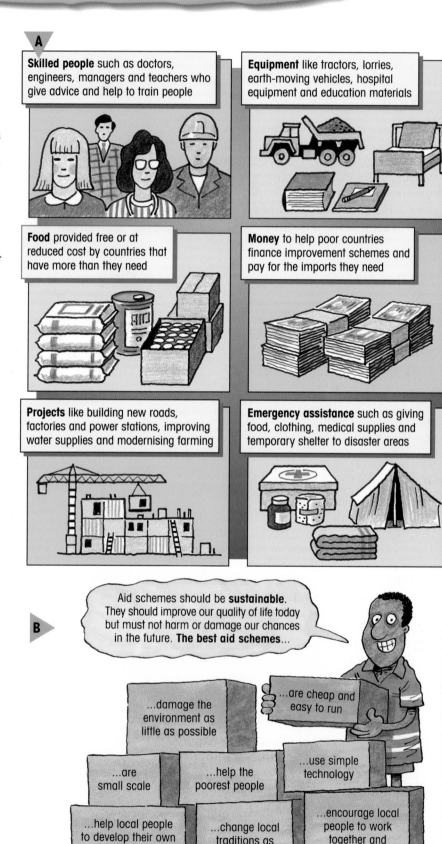

A

Skilled people such as doctors, engineers, managers and teachers who give advice and help to train people

Equipment like tractors, lorries, earth-moving vehicles, hospital equipment and education materials

Food provided free or at reduced cost by countries that have more than they need

Money to help poor countries finance improvement schemes and pay for the imports they need

Projects like building new roads, factories and power stations, improving water supplies and modernising farming

Emergency assistance such as giving food, clothing, medical supplies and temporary shelter to disaster areas

B Aid schemes should be **sustainable**. They should improve our quality of life today but must not harm or damage our chances in the future. **The best aid schemes...**

...damage the environment as little as possible

...are cheap and easy to run

...are small scale

...help the poorest people

...use simple technology

...help local people to develop their own knowledge and skills

...change local traditions as little as possible

...encourage local people to work together and help themselves

Activities

1 **a)** Draw a table and sort the newspaper headlines into two columns headed **Short-term aid** and **Long-term aid**.
  b) Choose two headlines from each column and suggest what aid might be most helpful to that country. Diagram **A** will help you.

2 **a)** Down the left hand side of your page write a list of six rules that you think all aid should keep to. Put them in the order you think most important. Diagram **B** will help you.
  b) Look at **C** below showing a water supply scheme in Kenya. For each rule, answer *Yes*, *No* or *Partly* to describe whether the scheme is keeping to that rule.
  c) Give the scheme a mark out of ten and write out a comment on its success.

> **Earthquake wrecks Mexico City**

> *Record debts hit Brazilian banks*

> *China seeks help for farming problems*

> **Crops lost in Bangladesh flood**

> **Water supply blamed for Ghana disaster**

> *Massive new health scheme planned for India*

C An example of **sustainable development**: a simple borehole well with a hand pump, which requires no servicing, supplies clean water to a small village in Kenya

- ◆ Simple **technology**; easy and cheap to run and repair
- ◆ Provides direct help for the people most in need
- ◆ Advisers help locals to make best use of new water supply
- ◆ Water supply can become a village meeting point
- ◆ Small-scale project with no bad effects on the environment
- ◆ Does not change local way of life

EXTRA

Imagine that you are to help organise the provision of a safe water supply to a country in Africa. Which eight of the following would be most useful to you? For each one that you choose, say how it would be used.

Money, farmer, drilling equipment, nurse, lorry, laboratory, water pipes, mechanic, tractor, water pump, chemist, geologist, teacher.

Summary

Aid is a form of help usually given by the wealthy areas of the world to the poorer areas. Aid schemes should be sustainable. If they are planned carefully they can help provide a better life for people living in poorer areas.

Should we give aid?

Aid comes from many different sources. In 1996 the British government gave around £2,300 million of aid to developing countries. **Charities** like Oxfam and Save the Children spent a total of over £100 million mainly funding small schemes and giving emergency aid. Large international organisations like the United Nations, the World Bank and the European Union provided more than £700 million of help to the poorer countries and regions of the world.

There are arguments as to whether we should give aid. Some people think that aid can be damaging and that people should help themselves. Others point out that we all live in the same world and we all rely on each other for our survival. We must therefore help each other and try, as far as possible, to improve the quality of life for everyone. What do *you* think? Look carefully at diagram **A** and try to decide whether we should or should not give aid.

A

Should we give aid?

A What's it got to do with us? We've got enough problems of our own.

B Without our help the poor people have no chance in life

C We should always help people who are worse off than ourselves

D Most aid is wasted or stolen and doesn't even get to the people who need it

E They are used to bad conditions. There's no need to help them.

F We all live in the same world. We should all help each other.

G The more aid we give, the less they will help themselves

H We need the things they have, so we might as well help them

I If we help the poorer countries it will provide new markets for our products

Activities

1 Look at diagram **A**.
   a) Give the letters of the speech bubbles that are:
   ● **for** giving aid
   ● **against** giving aid.
   b) Write out the two speech bubbles that you think are the best argument:
   ● **for** giving aid
   ● **against** giving aid.
   c) Do you think we should give more aid, less aid or no aid to people who live in countries that have a very low standard of living? Give reasons for your answer.

2 **a)** With a partner, play the game on the opposite page.
   ● Use a dice or spinner for each move.
   ● Follow the instructions for moves backwards or forwards.
   The winner is the first to reach the end of the road with the exact number.
   b) Play the game again. This time write down the **problems** and the **help** that you meet on the way. Do this in two columns. Underline the events which were affected by aid.

The road to development

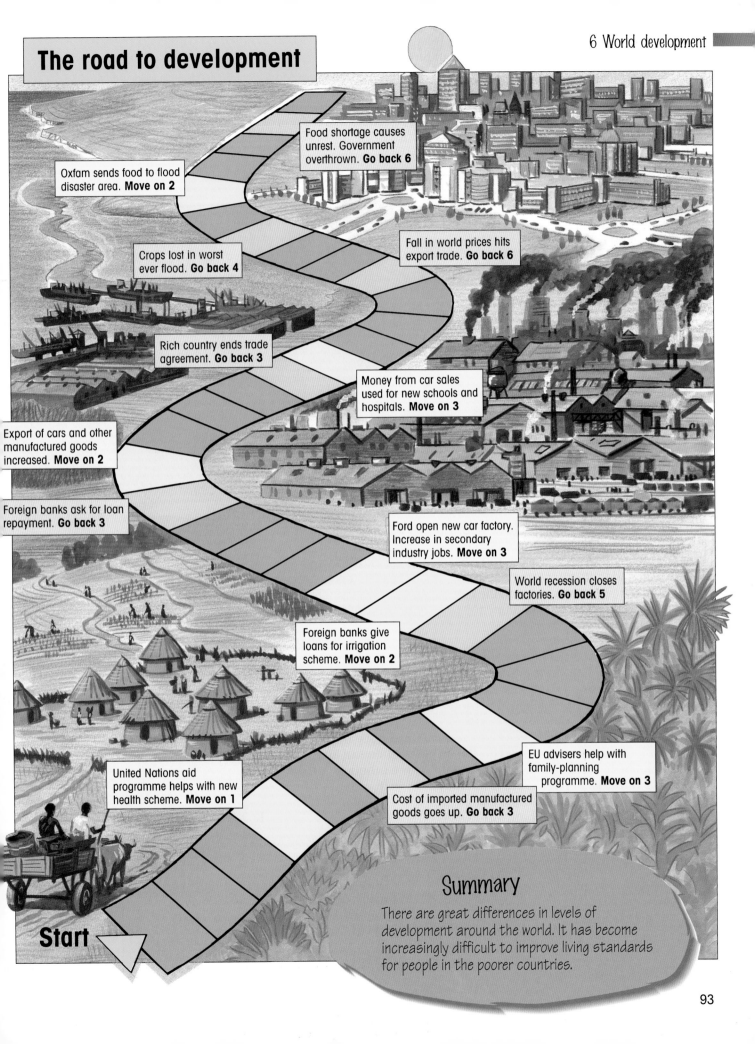

Oxfam sends food to flood disaster area. **Move on 2**

Food shortage causes unrest. Government overthrown. **Go back 6**

Crops lost in worst ever flood. **Go back 4**

Fall in world prices hits export trade. **Go back 6**

Rich country ends trade agreement. **Go back 3**

Money from car sales used for new schools and hospitals. **Move on 3**

Export of cars and other manufactured goods increased. **Move on 2**

Foreign banks ask for loan repayment. **Go back 3**

Ford open new car factory. Increase in secondary industry jobs. **Move on 3**

World recession closes factories. **Go back 5**

Foreign banks give loans for irrigation scheme. **Move on 2**

United Nations aid programme helps with new health scheme. **Move on 1**

Cost of imported manufactured goods goes up. **Go back 3**

EU advisers help with family-planning programme. **Move on 3**

Start

Summary

There are great differences in levels of development around the world. It has become increasingly difficult to improve living standards for people in the poorer countries.

The hazards enquiry

Over 40,000 earth tremors are recorded in California every year. In 1906 one of the most powerful earthquakes recorded this century devastated San Francisco. It caused 52 separate fires, destroyed over 28,000 buildings and killed nearly 1,000 people.

A

RUINS OF THE CITY AFTER EARTHQUAKE AND FIRE SAN FRANCISCO, CAL.

San Francisco is one of the most important and best known cities in the USA. It is located on a large bay in an attractive area of California and has become a prosperous and popular place to live. Unfortunately for the 5 million or so inhabitants of the area, San Francisco can also be a dangerous place to live because it lies in a very active earthquake zone.

Whilst earthquakes are too powerful and unpredictable for people to control them, careful planning can sometimes reduce the damage they cause.

In this enquiry you should imagine that you are a member of a team of earthquake experts based in San Francisco. You have been asked to write a report on the likely effects of a major earthquake on the city, and to suggest what could be done to reduce the earthquake threat.

You could work on the report by yourself, with a partner, or in a small group. You might be able to use a computer to word process your work and make it look more professional.

All the information that you need for the report can be found on pages 94–97, and in section 2 Hazards on pages 20–37. You may, though, like to research the topic using other books, the Internet, or any CD-ROMs to which you have access.

The main aims of the report are:
- to explain why earthquakes happen in San Francisco
- to identify which areas of the city may be most at risk, and describe what damage there could be
- to suggest what might be done to reduce the damaging effects of an earthquake on the city.

How is San Francisco affected by earthquakes, and what may be done to try to limit the damage caused?

B

Planners design buildings which they hope will withstand earthquakes. Tall steel-framed skyscrapers survive better than shorter concrete buildings. This is the Trans-America Pyramid, which was undamaged by the 1989 'quake.

1 Introduction – what is the enquiry about?

You will need to use maps and writing here. Star diagrams and labelled drawings might also help.

a) First say what your report will be about. The enquiry question and aims on page 94 will help you.

b) Next briefly describe San Francisco's main features. Points to consider:
- Where is it? (map, description)
- What is it like? (size, situation, importance)
- What is its earthquake history? (past 'quakes, damage)

c) Finally you could explain why earthquakes happen, and why San Francisco is particularly at risk. Pages 24–25, and the information in **D** below, will help you. Also mention why a plan is needed to help cope with the effects of an earthquake on such a large built-up area.

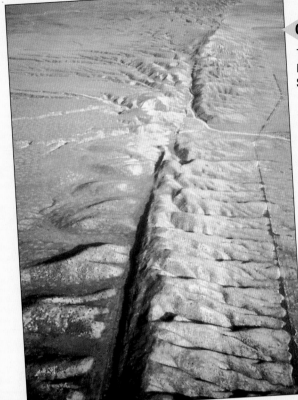

C

The San Andreas Fault south of San Francisco

D Geology of the San Francisco area

San Francisco lies close to the boundary of two giant plates. The plates move past each other causing friction and earth tremors. The boundary here is called the San Andreas fault.

Normally the movement is slight and only small earthquakes occur. Sometimes, though, as in 1906 and 1989, the plates become jammed and build up enormous pressure. When pressure is released there is a major earthquake.

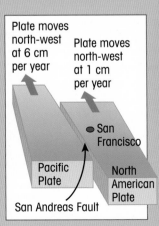

Plate moves north-west at 6 cm per year

Plate moves north-west at 1 cm per year

San Francisco

Pacific Plate

North American Plate

San Andreas Fault

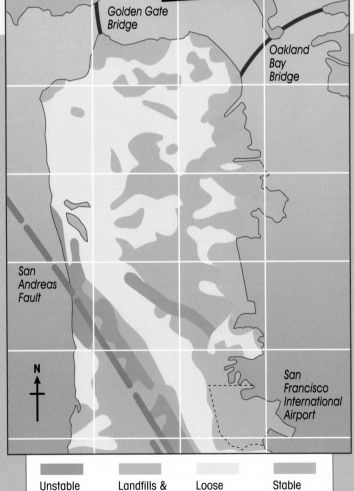

Golden Gate Bridge

Oakland Bay Bridge

San Andreas Fault

N

San Francisco International Airport

Unstable rock: *danger of landslides*	Landfills & soft muds: *danger of collapse*	Loose soils: *fairly stable*	Stable bedrock: *little movement*

Severe damage from earthquakes is most likely to happen close to the San Andreas Fault.

However, the nature of the ground also affects how much damage might occur. Areas of solid, stable bedrock tend to suffer less damage than places with unstable rock, soft sands or newly filled land.

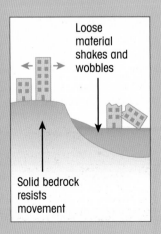

Loose material shakes and wobbles

Solid bedrock resists movement

2 What could be the effects of an earthquake?

a) Areas at risk

- First look closely at maps **D**, **F**, **G** and **H** and decide which parts of the city you think could suffer the most damage in a future earthquake.
- Next describe where these places are and give reasons for your decisions. You could use a labelled map or sketch, and writing, here.

b) Possible damage

- Using maps **F**, **G** and **H**, assess the damage that might happen at the six numbered locations on map **H**. Write your answers on a larger copy of table **E**.
- Choose some or all of the labelled locations on map **H** and suggest how they might be affected by an earthquake. What impact would these effects have on the city as a whole?

E Damage assessment survey

Location from map H	Possible damage – serious, moderate, or very little	Reason
1		
2		
3		
4		
5		
6		

F 1906 earthquake damage

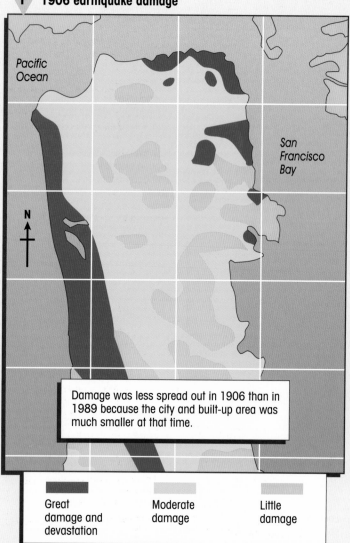

Damage was less spread out in 1906 than in 1989 because the city and built-up area was much smaller at that time.

Great damage and devastation   Moderate damage   Little damage

G Ground shaking prediction

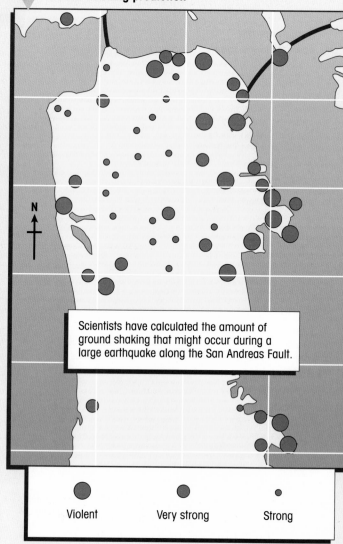

Scientists have calculated the amount of ground shaking that might occur during a large earthquake along the San Andreas Fault.

Violent   Very strong   Strong

San Francisco today ▶ **H**

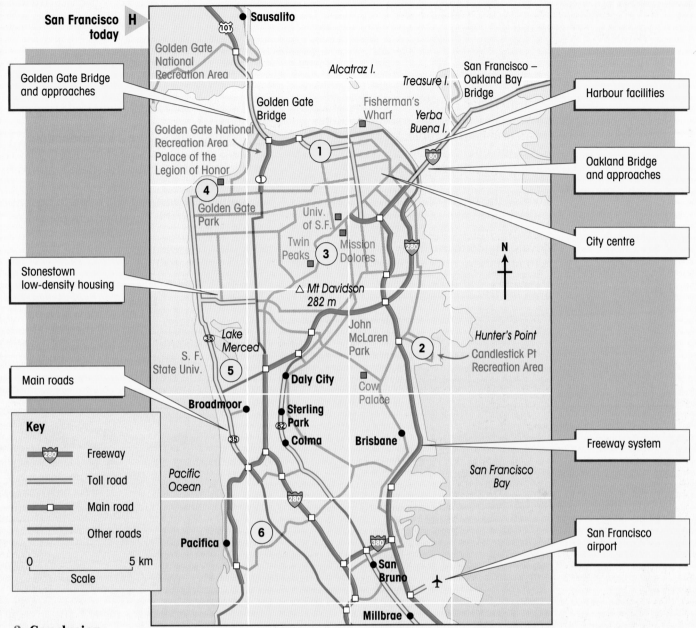

Golden Gate Bridge and approaches

Golden Gate National Recreation Area

Golden Gate National Recreation Area Palace of the Legion of Honor

Stonestown low-density housing

Main roads

Harbour facilities

Oakland Bridge and approaches

City centre

Freeway system

San Francisco airport

Key

🛡280	Freeway
	Toll road
▭	Main road
	Other roads

0 — 5 km
Scale

Sausalito · Alcatraz I. · Treasure I. · San Francisco – Oakland Bay Bridge · Golden Gate Bridge · Fisherman's Wharf · Yerba Buena I. · Univ. of S.F. · Twin Peaks · Mission Dolores · △ Mt Davidson 282 m · John McLaren Park · Hunter's Point · Candlestick Pt Recreation Area · Lake Merced · S. F. State Univ. · Daly City · Cow Palace · Broadmoor · Sterling Park · Colma · Brisbane · San Francisco Bay · Pacific Ocean · Pacifica · San Bruno · Millbrae

3 Conclusion

There could be two parts to this, and together they should answer the enquiry question.

a) First give a brief summary of what you have said in the main part of your report. You could do this with a simple 'cause and effect' diagram, or a few brief paragraphs of writing.

b) Secondly, you should suggest what planners might do to try to limit earthquake damage. Some questions you might consider are:

- Where should rescue services be located?
- Which areas might best be suited to parks and open spaces?
- What activities should be kept away from high-risk areas?
- How can building design help limit damage?
- What emergency preparation could help reduce the earthquake threat?

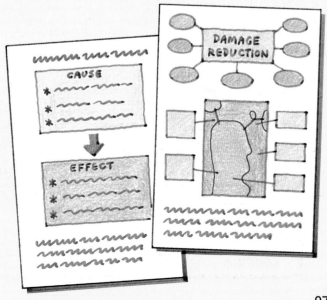

The tourism enquiry

Tourism is one of the world's fastest growing industries. It can bring benefits but it can also cause problems. This enquiry is about the effects that tourism can have on an area in northern England.

Look at the photo opposite which shows a valley in the Lake District National Park. A holiday company has shown interest in developing tourism in the valley. Your task is to plan these developments, and suggest what effects they will have on the local area.

How can the development of tourism affect areas of great scenic attraction?

There should be three main parts to your enquiry.
- The first part will be an introduction. Here you should say what the enquiry is about, and describe the main features of the area.
- In the next part you will need to describe and explain the development plans for the valley.
- Finally you will need to outline the good points and the bad points of the scheme, and give your considered opinion on it.

It will be best if you can work with a partner or in a small group. You will then be able to share views and discuss ideas with each other. You will find pages 39–45 of this book helpful as you work through the enquiry.

1 Introduction – what is the enquiry about?

You could use maps, sketches, lists, writing or star diagrams here.

a) First look carefully at the enquiry question and the guidelines given at the top of page 98. Say briefly what you have to do and how you are going to do it.

b) Next show where the Lake District National Park is located. The map on page 43 will help you.

c) Now describe the main features of the valley as it is today. Use the photo below and information in the drawing opposite. A labelled sketch could be useful here.

d) Explain why the valley seems to be a good place for tourist development.

Proposals

1 Hotel

Either by itself or including indoor and outdoor sports facilities

2 Holiday chalets

Either one, two, or three groups: ten chalets and a small shop in each group

3 Campsite & log cabins

Either one or two for cheaper accommodation

4 Car parks

Either one, two, or three car parks with toilets

5 Shops

Either one, two, or three souvenir shops with cafés

6 Water park

Buildings and facilities for water sports (decision needed on whether to allow power boats)

7 Roads

Additional access roads where required

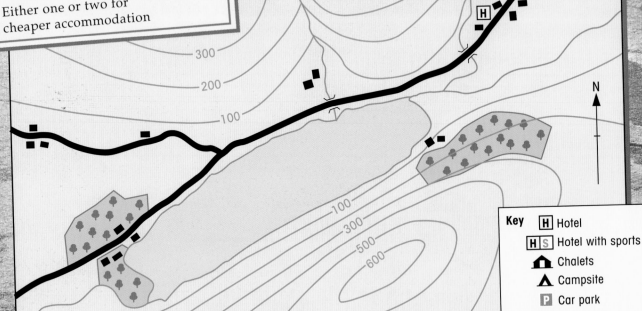

Key
H	Hotel
H S	Hotel with sports
	Chalets
	Campsite
P	Car park
W	Water park
	Road
	Trees

2 What will the development be like?

Look carefully at the proposals on the opposite page. They are designed to attract families with a broad range of interests and varying levels of wealth. Discuss with your partner or group what developments you wish to have, where they will go, and what they will look like. You can add other features of your choice if you wish.

Remember that your plans will need to be accepted by the National Park Planning Board. You should therefore consider very carefully the views of the park ranger on page 98.

a) On a copy of the map, mark your plans for the valley. Use the symbols in the key, and be as accurate as possible.

b) Describe and give reasons for your proposals. Mention any special points such as the positioning of features, materials to be used, and possible landscaping.

3 Conclusion

Now you must look carefully at your work and answer the enquiry question. Notice that it begins 'How . . . '. That means you will need to both describe your findings, and explain them.

a) First you will need to make a summary of how the valley might change if it were developed for tourism.

b) Next you should list the good points and the bad points of the development. In doing this you should consider the local people, the tourists and the environment.

c) Finally you might like to decide whether the valley should be left in its present state or developed according to your suggestions. If it were developed, how could planning and management help to increase the good effects but reduce the bad ones? Page 42 will help you here.

Now how can we change all this... or do we really want to?

Let's make sure we get the balance right!

RANGER

TOURISM

GOOD

BAD

Glossary

A

Active volcano	A volcano that has erupted recently and is likely to erupt again. *20, 22, 68, 69*
Adapt	Plants and animals which have learnt to live with the temperatures and rainfall of an area. *10, 11, 14, 15, 18*
Aid	Help usually given by the richer countries of the world to the poorer ones. It may be short-term aid such as food given for an emergency, or long-term aid such as training in health care. *90–93*
Altitude	The height of a place above sea-level. *9*
Ash and dust	Fine material thrown out by a volcano. *20, 21*

B

Buttress roots	Roots which stand above the ground to support large trees. *10*

C

Cactus	A plant that grows in dry areas and is able to store water in its stem or roots. *14*
Canopy	An almost unbroken top layer of trees which acts like a roof over the tropical rainforest. *10, 11*
Charities	Voluntary organisations that provide help for those in need. *90–93*
CIS	The Commonwealth of Independent States are twelve of the fifteen former states of the USSR which became independent in 1991 but still group together. *68–71*
Clay	A finely-grained substance that easily sticks together and is found is most types of soil. *30, 31*
Climate	The weather of a place taken on average over many years. *4–9, 12, 13, 16, 17, 63, 72*
Commercial farming	When farm produce is sold for a profit. *64*
Conflict	Disagreement over the use of resources. *44, 45*
Conservationist	A person who believes in protecting and preserving animals, plants, buildings, environments, etc. *44, 45*
Convectional rainfall	Rain that is produced when air is made to rise by surface warming. *6, 12*
Core	The central part of the earth. *28*
Crater	A roughly circular bowl-shaped opening in a volcano. *20*
Crust	The outer layer of the earth. *28*

D

Deforestation	The clearing and destruction of forests. Deforestation may lead to soil erosion. *18, 35, 62*
Delta	A flat area of fertile land formed at the mouth of a river. *62*
Development	How rich or poor a country is compared with other areas. It can be measured in many different ways. *84 and Unit 6*
Dormant plants	Vegetation which is inactive and not actually growing at a particular time. *14,18*
Dormant volcano	A volcano that has erupted within historic times (in the last 2,000 years) but not recently. *20*
Drought	A long spell of dry weather. *14, 16, 18, 63, 66*

E

Earthquakes	A movement or tremor of the earth's crust. *24–29, 62, 68, 69*
Economic activities	Primary, secondary or tertiary (service) jobs. *38, 64, 66, 71, 86, 87*
Employment structure	The proportion of people working in primary, secondary and tertiary industries. *64, 66, 86, 87*
Equatorial climate	Places near to the Equator which are hot and wet throughout the year. *8, 9*
European Union	A group of fifteen European countries working together for the benefit of everyone. *54, 55*
Evergreen	Trees which always have some green leaves growing throughout the year. *10, 18*
Exports	Goods sold to other countries. *71, 88, 89, 93*
Extinct volcano	A volcano that has not erupted in historic times and is not expected to erupt again. *20*

F

Flow map	A map showing how many people or things move from one place to another. *47*

	Fossil fuels	Fuels like coal, oil and gas formed from the remains of animals and plants millions of years ago. Fossil fuels give off carbon dioxide gas when burnt and are non-renewable. *36*
	Frontal rain	When warm air is forced to rise over cold air, usually in a depression. *6*
G	**Geothermal**	Energy obtained from the hot rocks found under the earth's surface. *74*
	Global warming	Worldwide warming of the atmosphere due to increases in the amount of carbon dioxide and other gases being released into the atmosphere by the burning of fossil fuels. *36, 37*
	Greenhouse effect	The way the atmosphere traps some of the sun's heat to warm our environment. *36, 37*
H	**Habitat**	The environment or natural home of plants and animals. *79*
	Hazard	Something that is a problem or a danger to people. *22–37, 63*
	Hot deserts	Places which have very little rain or vegetation. *12–15*
	Humus	Remains of plants and animals left in the soil. *31*
	Hydro-electricity	Energy obtained from using fast-flowing water. *65, 74*
I	**Imports**	Goods brought into a country. *71, 88, 89, 93*
	Infrared photograph	Photos obtained from satellites which, as they go round the earth, record the amount of heat (radiation) given off from different surfaces. *59, 80*
	Intensive farming	Farms which are often small in size but use either many people or a lot of machines. No land is wasted. *64, 78*
L	**Latitude**	How far a place is north or south of the Equator. *4, 6, 9, 13, 17, 68, 69*
	Lava	Molten rock flowing out of the ground, usually from a volcano. *20, 21*
	Lianas	Vine-like plants which climb up the trunks of trees. *10*
	Life expectancy	The average number of years a person can expect to live. *70*
	Living standards	A measure of the quality of people's lives. *84, 85*
M	**Magma**	Molten rock below the earth's surface. *20, 29*
	Magma chamber	Where molten lava is found deep below the earth's surface *20*
	Mantle	The layer of the earth below the crust and above the core. *28, 29*
	Manufactured goods	Secondary industry products such as cars, machinery and electrical goods. They are usually of high value. *76, 88, 89, 93*
	Mediterranean climate	Places which have hot, dry summers and mild, wet winters. *16, 17, 58, 63*
	Migration	The movement of people from one place to another. *56, 65–67*
N	**National Park**	An area of beautiful countryside preserved by law from development. *42–45, 79*
	Natural hazard	A great force of nature, such as an earthquake or volcano, which is a threat or a danger to people. *22, 72*
	Natural vegetation	Vegetation which has not been affected by human activity. *10, 14, 18, 19, 62, 79*
	Nocturnal	Wildlife that is only active at night. *15*
	Non-renewable	Resources that can only be used once, e.g. coal and oil. *74*
	Nuclear power	Energy obtained from uranium. *74, 75*
O	**One-child families**	A method of reducing population growth by encouraging parents to limit their family size to one child. *84, 85*
	Overgrazing	Damaging pasture by keeping too many animals on it. Overgrazing may lead to soil erosion. *32, 35*
	Overpopulated	When there are more people living in an area than the area can support. *84*
P	**Park ranger**	A person employed by the National Parks Authorities. They help visitors enjoy the Parks and ensure that the landscape is protected. *42, 43*
	Peninsula	A piece of land surrounded on three sides by the sea. *56, 58*
	Plain	A low-lying flat area of land. *56, 62, 63, 64, 65*
	Plate boundary	The place where plates meet. *28, 29*
	Plates	Large sections of the earth's crust *28, 29*
	Pollution	Noise, dust and other harmful substances produced by people and machines, which spoil an area. *36, 37, 40, 41, 80, 81*
	Population density	The number of people living in a given area. It is a measure of how crowded a place is. *70*

	Prevailing winds	The direction from which the wind usually comes. *4, 5, 6, 9, 12, 16*
	Primary goods	Raw materials such as minerals, timber and foodstuffs. They are usually of low value. *64, 66, 88, 89*
	Primary occupations	Work which involves people taking raw materials from the natural environment. *38, 86, 87*
Q	**Quality of life**	A measure of a person's wellbeing – how happy and content they are with their life-style and physical surroundings. *84*
R	**Region**	An area of land with similar characteristics, e.g. relief, climate, political, economic activities. *60, 61*
	Relief	The shape and height of the land. *4, 5, 9, 59, 68, 69*
	Relief rain	Rain caused by air being forced to rise over hills and mountains. *5, 6, 16*
	Renewable	Resources that can be used over and over again. *74*
	Resources	Things which can be useful to people. They can be natural like iron and coal or of other value like money and skilled workers. *84*
	'Ring of fire'	A circle of volcanoes around the edge of the Pacific Ocean. *26*
	River basin	An area of land drained by a river and its tributaries. *68, 69*
S	**Sand**	A gritty, fine material that is found in most types of soil. *30*
	Satellite image	Pictures of the earth taken by satellites. The images can show either true or false colours. *59, 80*
	Scrub	Small, stunted trees and bushes. *18, 19, 58, 62*
	Secondary industries	Where people are employed to make or manufacture something from raw materials. *38, 64, 66, 86, 87*
	Seismograph	An instrument used to measure earthquakes. *27*
	Self-help scheme	Where local people are involved in improving conditions for themselves, e.g. schemes to prevent or reduce soil erosion. *35*
	Service	Something that is provided to meet people's needs. *38*
	Shrub layer	The lowest of three layers of plants growing in the tropical rainforests. *10*
	Silt	Material deposited by a river. A type of soil with a smooth feel to it. *30, 62*
	Soil	The loose material on the earth's surface in which plants grow. *30–33*
	Soil erosion	The wearing away and loss of soil mainly due to wind, rain and running water. *32, 33, 34, 35*
	Soil organic content	The remains of plant and animal life in a soil. *30, 31*
	Soil texture	How soil feels to the touch. It may be sticky, smooth or gritty. *30, 31*
	Species	Groups of plants and animals. *11, 79*
	Subsistence farming	Growing just enough food for your own needs and having virtually nothing left over to sell. *66*
	Sustainable development	A method of progress that does not waste resources, and looks after the needs of today without damaging resources for the future. *90, 91*
T	**Terracing**	A flat shelf cut into a hillside and used for growing crops. *35, 58, 78*
	Tertiary industry	An industry that provides a service for people. Teachers, shop assistants and tourist industry workers are in this type of industry. *38, 64, 66, 86, 87*
	Tourism	When people travel to places for recreation and pleasure. *38 and Unit 3*
	Trade	The exchange of goods between people or countries. *55, 71, 88–91*
	Tropical rainforests	Tall, dense forests found in hot, wet climates. *10, 11*
	Tsunamis	Tidal waves caused by undersea earthquakes. *72, 75*
	Typhoons	Storms with very strong winds and heavy rainfall. *72*
U	**Under-canopy**	The middle of the three layers of trees growing in the tropical rainforests. *10*
V	**Vent**	An opening in the earth's surface through which material is forced during a volcanic eruption. *20*
	Volcano	A cone-shaped mountain or hill often made up from lava and ash. *20–23, 26, 28, 29, 56, 58, 68, 69*
	Volcanic bombs	Large rock fragments thrown out by an erupting volcano. *20*
W	**Weather**	The day-to-day state of the atmosphere. It includes temperature, rainfall and wind. *4, 5, 8*
Z	**Zones of activity**	Areas where earthquakes and volcanoes are common. *27*